THE LAST ONE

LEAVING

MAYBERRY

PLEASE TURN OUT THE LIGHTS

AN APPALACHIAN ANTHOLOGY

Aaron McAlexander

With contributions from Yeatts Family Members

ISBN-13-978-0-615-47720-6

Dedicated to my lovely wife
Glenda
Who is happy to be in her studio potting while I am in my cave writing.

ISBN-13 978-0-615-47720-6

Fourth Printing

Printed in the U.S.A.

CONTENTS

Prologue

Many folks are unaware that there is a real community by the name of "Mayberry" in the mountains of southwestern Virginia, and that it has been there, nestled on the southeastern rim of the Blue Ridge Plateau, for about one hundred and fifty years. I overheard a conversation at the *Mayberry Trading Post* a while back that brought home this point.

"I'm surprised they let you use that name on your store," commented the customer, obviously a tourist, as he paid for his purchases.

"I'm not sure who you mean by *they*," replied the lady behind the counter, in her warm, Southwestern Virginia accent. "But **Mayberry** was on the front of this store here for about seventy years before it ever showed up on television."

For the past twenty years, I have spent about half of my time in the community of Mayberry, Virginia. I spent most of my formative years in Meadows of Dan, about four miles to the north of Mayberry. My mother was born in Mayberry, spent her childhood there, and *her* mother was born in Mayberry and lived there her entire life.

My maternal great-grandmother moved there with her family in 1878, when my grandfather was eight years old. By that time, the community had been known as either *Mayberry Creek* or *Mayberry* since sometime before the civil war. My grandpa was once the mail carrier for the United States Post Office in Mayberry, and he delivered mail by horse and buggy over a thirty mile route that included my paternal grandparents as patrons.

If you would like to visit Mayberry, Virginia, I suggest that you not wait around too long, for there are but a few surviving reminders of this once thriving community, and the number of native citizens is in rapid decline. The post office, the school, the blacksmith shop, and the tannery are all long gone, while the bed and breakfast and the real estate office have both closed within the last couple of years. Like so many small, culturally rich, rural communities in America, Mayberry has been decimated by time and economics. The original *Old Mayberry* was a community of small farms, each supplying a family with most of its basic material needs. The few small businesses clustered around the intersection of what were once Mayberry Road and Rorrer Road furnished the rest. Today, most residents of Mayberry enjoying any steady employment other than farming must commute.

Around 1900, approximately fifty families – about three hundred souls – called Mayberry their home. The population had begun to decline somewhat around the nineteen twenties, but it experienced a temporary resurgence in the thirties. In nineteen thirty-five, the City of Danville began the Pinnacles Hydroelectric Development Project, a municipal undertaking that resulted in the construction of two dams and a hydroelectric power plant on the Dan River. Two years later, construction began on the Blue Ridge Parkway, the first paved road through Mayberry. These Federally sponsored government projects during the Roosevelt Administration created a level of activity in Mayberry which exceeded anything known there before or since. Mayberry residents of a generation or two back would sometimes joke about how, during the thirties, folks in Mayberry were mostly unaware that they were supposed to be in the Great Depression; the blight that wiped out the chestnut orchards had a more serious impact on the local economy.

Seventy years ago, most of the farms in and around Mayberry were stocked with sheep, cattle, pigs, and chickens. Most residents generated an income from the sale of livestock, eggs, and milk. Now, only one large dairy farm still operates in Mayberry, but its milk production is several times that of all of the local farms of a few years ago combined.

Of the Mayberry residents who commute to work, some also raise beef cattle and crops such as cabbage or pumpkins on family land as a second source of income. The only remaining business establishment in Mayberry is the *Mayberry Trading Post*, formerly the *Mayberry Store*. The Mayberry Community of today is pretty much defined by the *Trading Post* (Established in 1893) and the Presbyterian Church (Established in 1925).

Mayberry, Virginia, is located on a plateau in the Southern Blue Ridge Mountains at an elevation of nearly 3000 feet. With the exception of the southern rim, where the Appalachian Plateau abruptly drops off onto the piedmont below, the mountains in Mayberry are more accurately described as hills. It is a land of forested hills footed by streams Mayberry Creek, Round Meadow Creek, and Haunted Branch – all flowing into the Dan River near the brink of the plateau. Much of Mayberry proper is located along Mayberry Church Road, a road which runs almost parallel to the section of the Blue Ridge Parkway between mileposts 178 and 182.

I don't usually have a lot to say about my connections to the mountain Mayberry. That's because if I mention it, folks just naturally assume that I am referring to Mount Airy, North Carolina. Mt. Airy is arguably the model for the *Mayberry* of the popular 1960's television series, *The Andy Griffith Show*. Some folks might even be offended if I tell them that my origins are in the "original Mayberry." I love *both* Mayberrys, so allow me to declare myself to be one of *The Andy Griffith Show's* most devoted fans. It is certainly possible, however, or even likely, that Andy Griffith, who grew up in Mt. Airy, North Carolina, may have gotten the name of his television town from Mayberry, Virginia. It is only about twenty miles from Mount Airy to Mayberry (if you take Squirrel Spur Road, it may seem a bit farther). Some of the show's characters, Otis Campbell and Earnest T. Bass in particular, strongly remind me of Mayberry locals whom I recall as frequenting The Mayberry Store when I was a child. But then, every place has it colorful residents.

The Mayberry of television, along with Mount Airy and Andy Griffith, belong to North Carolina, and I have no desire to detract from that connection. The Mount Airy of today is one of the few small towns I can name which has a booming downtown district, convenient parking, all of the downtown store fronts occupied, and shoppers bustling in and out all day long. Much of the vitality of downtown Mount Airy has to be because of the successful association of the television town of Mayberry with the real town of Mount Airy, North Carolina.

As a loyal fan of the Andy Griffith show, I hope it continues to be syndicated for another fifty years. On the other hand, my mountain Mayberry lineage extends from my great-grandmother, through grandparents and parents, and forward to my grandchildren, who think Mayberry, Virginia, is truly a wonderful place. My mother and her seven siblings were born and reared in Mayberry, and either an uncle or a cousin operated the Mayberry Store for about sixty years. Cousins still occupy and maintain the old family home in Mayberry.

It is a cliché, I know, but whether or not folks consider themselves to be residents of Mayberry appears to largely be a state of mind. From the center of the community of Mayberry, towards Meadows of Dan to the north, towards Bellspur to the south, or towards Laurel Fork to the west, whether a local individual claims to be a resident of Mayberry or some other of the surrounding communities appears to be determined by family history. And there are many of us who think that being a resident of Mayberry is something of which one should be proud.

Today, the existence of the "Mountain Mayberry" is obscured by the fact that there is no longer a Mayberry post office address; for many years now, Mayberry and many other nearby communities have been a part of the rural route system served by the post office at Meadows of Dan, Virginia. Many other nearby post office communities such as Tobax, Ballard, Keno, and Cruise have completely disappeared except from the minds of the few residents who maintain a historical interest.

This collection of family stories, vignettes from life in Mayberry over a span of six generations, is my personal attempt to keep the memory and spirit of the *Mountain Mayberry* alive for a while longer. I'm sure that some of my friends and family who read this collection of family stories will want to know why I didn't include *their* favorite Mayberry story. Just a while back, a friend who was reading this collection of tales for me wanted to know, "Why didn't you include the story about the time the preacher found the opossum in the narthex?" Well, I hadn't heard that story before, but I did write it down. There are probably enough interesting tales about life in the mountain Mayberry for many volumes.

Aaron McAlexander

The Move to Mayberry

"We were just sitting down for supper when I heard the wagon coming up the road. I could tell that Muh was real upset, but she just said, 'Oh, Lordy Mercy! Children, just go on and eat.' Then she walked out and met the wagon as it pulled to a stop in front of the house."

"We could hear that Muh and the man driving the wagon talking real seriously about something, and finally Muh says, 'Well, come on then, and let's get started.' That's when she came back into the house and announced that we were going to have to leave this house and that were going to move to Mayberry. While the man unhitched the horses Muh sat back down at the table, but she just couldn't eat. Then the man came on into the house."

"I had never seen the man before, but Muh told us that he was our Uncle Cab and that he was here to help us move. Little Muh, all upset, started flitting around the room, giving everybody orders. 'Etta, clear off the table. George, you and Dump pull the drawers out of the big chest. George, help Cab tote the chest out to the wagon.' I had never seen her like that."

"Muh made it clear that we were going to pack everything into the wagon now and we would be leaving before daylight. Later she told us why she wanted for us to leave so early. She said, 'I was afraid that if I looked back and could see the home place, sitting there beside the river, my heart just might break right then.' Anyway, she knew that the trip to Mayberry was going to take all of a very long day, and we needed an early start." Although Grandpa was only eight at the time, he always said that he could remember the day they moved "up the mountain" as clearly as any day of his life.

John Henry Yeatts, the chubby little boy who would one day become my grandfather, was born to Henry and Caron Yeatts of Taylorsville, Virginia in eighteen seventy. His mother, who was called "Muh" by her children, called him her "little dumpling." His older siblings soon shortened it to "Dump," and it became the nickname he would be stuck with for the remainder of his ninety-seven years.

When first told that they would have to leave, Caron Yeatts had no idea what her family was going to do. Muh knew her father owned some land in Mayberry and in her distraught state, she began talking about borrowing the neighbor's ox cart and hitching it to the cow to move their few belongings to Mayberry. Fortunately, Muh found someone with a horse and wagon who was willing to move the family and their belongings up the mountain to Mayberry. When he was in his nineties, Grandpa could still describe in detail how the man, Grandpa thought he was an uncle – either a Cab or a Cal Boswell – brought his horse and wagon down from Floyd the day before the move, and had spent the night so they could leave really early the next morning.

Little Muh was a tiny woman who made up in energy and determination what she lacked in size. She got up long before daybreak on that late June morning in 1878, and was soon bustling around getting everyone else moving. Most of the few pieces of furniture had been loaded into the wagon the night before, so they spent the night sleeping on pallets on the floor. In the morning, they sat in a circle around the lamp on the floor eating from a bowl of cornmeal mush, and while Muh and the man drank black coffee, the children drank the last of the fresh milk. Muh carefully packed all of the food they had left for the long day's journey into the wagon: a few flour biscuits, a crock of buttermilk, and a wooden bucket filled with June apples. Henrietta, the oldest child, rinsed out the coffee pot and the bowls in the spring, then packed them away. The last of their belongings were piled into the wagon, and they were on their way.

"We were a sad little procession," described Grandpa, "plodding through Taylorsville in the dark, past the stores and the bank, and out onto the Trot Valley Road. There was not one light to be seen anywhere until just before the sun began to rise. The man sat on the front of the wagon driving the horse, but the rest of us all started out walking. The wagon led the way, with the cow trailing along behind it, led by a short rope. Muh and Tobe followed, then Etta and George, while I was left tagging along at the rear. Whenever anyone spoke, it was in a hushed voice, as though we wished to not attract attention to the fact that we had to leave our home. It felt like we were being banished."

There wasn't enough room in the wagon for everybody. "Tobe was just a little feller, and George was kind of lame, so Muh, Tobe and George all climbed up into the wagon soon as we got onto the Trot Valley Road. By that time we had already walked about three miles. Some of us took turns riding in the wagon through the valley, but when we turned up the Rye Cove Road, the way got really steep. We had to make it easier on the horse, so everybody but little Tobe and Uncle Cab got out and walked. Before long, we were all feeling tired and getting hungry, but Muh announced that there wouldn't be anything to eat until we got to the top of the mountain. That sounded pretty discouraging to me, since it was still morning, and I knew we wouldn't get to the top of the mountain for a long time. When I asked how much farther it was to Mayberry, I was told "about twenty miles." Lucky for me, I had no idea how far that really was."

In the years following the American Civil War, thousands of Southern families, their sons and fathers having lost their lives or their health in defense of the Confederate Cause, also lost their farms and homes. For many of the traditional Southern aristocracy, converting from the old plantation system using slave labor to a similar system using sharecropper labor seemed like nothing more than a sound economic plan. When a farm was lost to foreclosure, the lender would usually soon sell it to a planter for a fraction of its pre-war value. The farm family was often allowed to remain on the land, with the farmer working as a sharecropper for the new owner. If a sharecropping family lacked the manpower to operate the farm profitably, then they would soon be moved out, and this is what happened to the family of Henry and Caron Yeatts.

Henry Faison Yeatts, originally from Pittsylvania County, had married Caron Boswell from Franklin County, Virginia in 1860. The couple was living in the foothills of the Blue Ridge Mountains of southwestern Virginia, just southeast of what was then Taylorsville, near the Mayo River. Henry was successfully farming a "nice piece" of fertile bottomland, when the Civil War began. Unlike many of the young men in the region, Henry Yeatts did not immediately volunteer for the Confederate Army. The household in which he was raised belonged to the Church of the Brethren. That faith, an offshoot of the Methodist Church and although not actively abolitionist, was basically opposed to slavery. His wife, Caron, was of the same faith, so it is unlikely that Henry ever had any aspirations to become a slave holder. Later in the war, with the Southern

Cause in decline, Henry Yeatts felt compelled by his loyalty to Virginia to join the Confederate Army and was assigned to the 34th Virginia Militia. Because Henry was a farmer, skilled in working with horses and mules, he spent most of his time in the Confederate Army as a "mule skinner" and wagoner. He was never injured in battle, but he did contract one of the many illnesses which pervaded the military camps in the war, and he very nearly died. (About twice as many Confederate soldiers died in service from disease as died from enemy action.) At the end of the war, Henry Yeatts returned to his Southwestern Virginia farm a "broken man," to use a common phrase of the day. Although he lived on for several more years, he was chronically ill and was never able to work hard enough to make the farm prosper, even with the help of his hard-working wife and older children.

In April of 1870, five months before the birth of his son John Henry, Henry F. Yeatts died, leaving his widow with three young children and a burden of debt. Caron was able to earn a little money by taking in boarders, as she and the older children continued to try growing corn and tobacco on the farm. Even in the dismal economy of the reconstruction, Muh and the children managed to hold on to the farm for a few more years, but the South was in an economic depression throughout most of the eighteen seventies, and in 1878, the inevitable occurred. The bank sold the house and the land, forcing the destitute family out of their home.

Caron Yeatts and her family moving to Mayberry may have partially been associated with Caron's having given birth to another child, Charles Tobias, in eighteen seventy-five. The standards of that time and place would have meant that any widow having a child several years after her husband's death would have been branded an immoral woman. Grandpa thought that the father of the child was probably a doctor who had boarded with the family for an extended period of time and who possibly had helped to support them. My own mother, who could be very judgmental about some things, always defended Muh, declaring that "she did what she had to do to feed her hungry children." Muh may have hoped they could start a new life in Mayberry, but she probably didn't expect much beyond their bare survival.

Early in June of 1878, Muh and her four children left the bottomland farm beside the Mayo River and headed up and into the Blue Ridge Mountains to the remote community of Mayberry, Virginia. Muh's parents, Jane and Mark Boswell had moved to Mayberry from Franklin County several years before, and it would have doubtlessly been helpful for her to be near them, but Muh probably had no idea of the primitive conditions they would face in the place to which they were moving. When Mark and Jane Boswell first moved to Mayberry, they had built a tiny cabin on Mayberry Creek. They lived on a parcel of land to which no one had officially laid claim for over seven years, allowing them to homestead land which had once belonged to an earlier settler, probably Steptoe Langhorne. When Mark Boswell petitioned the state and no one came forth to object, he was granted the land under the Virginia Homestead Act. Muh's folks had later moved on to a better farm and with a more comfortable cabin. Now Muh and her family were told that they could move into the old one.

The one small, horse-drawn wagon held everything Muh and her family owned. There was the large round-top steamer trunk which Henry and Caron had been given on their wedding day. It now held every stitch of their clothing that Muh or the children were not wearing, plus several bed quilts. A wooden box contained their a few cooking pots and the coal-oil lantern, which was surely precious to them. Grandpa Henry's squirrel rifle, wrapped up in an old quilt, was carefully stashed in the bottom of the wagon. But it was the contents of the wooden rain barrel that was truly essential to the family's survival. It held their few farming implements and Henry Yeatts's blacksmithing tools.

Carefully wrapped in a wet tow sack and stuffed in the barrel among the tools were sprouts that Muh had cut from the Yellow Transparent and Virginia Beauty apple trees. Wherever they went, if Muh could find a volunteer apple tree on which to graft those sprouts, they would someday maybe have their favorite apples.

Their furniture consisted of one large and very old maple chest of drawers, a home-built table with its four cane bottomed chairs, a three-legged stool, and an old church bench. There was also the bedstead, along with its trundle bed and three straw-filled ticks. A bucket, initially filled with water, was hung from a stanchion on the side of the wagon, but it soon had sloshed out most of its contents. A coop containing their few chickens was tied onto the tailgate, with the bony heifer pulled along behind the wagon completing the inventory.

It was dark when the exhausted family finally arrived at the cabin on Mayberry Creek, leaving little that could be done that evening except for watering the cow and the horse and staking them out where they could get some grass, and feeding and watering the chickens in their coop. Finally, they unrolled the straw ticks onto the dirt floor of the cabin, where they collapsed into sleep in a strange and total darkness.

The Mayberry cabin was built of rough, unhewn logs chinked with mud. It consisted of but a single room with a dirt floor, a sleeping loft overhead, and a lean-to expansion tacked onto one side. The original builder had used the only really level spot in the narrow valley, placing the cabin about twenty feet from the creek. Except for narrow strips of bottom land running along either side of the creek, the land surrounding the cabin was steep and rocky, extending upwards on both sides away from the creek bottom. Grandpa once described how, the morning after they arrived, he walked outside and looked around at his new home. Even at his young age, he concluded that they would probably starve there.

There were only a few acres of barely farmable land in the place where they found themselves, and soon there were only Muh and the children to farm that rocky hollow. The oldest child, Henrietta, called "Etta," had turned seventeen and left to work at the cotton mills in Danville. But George Preston was fourteen and, in spite of being somewhat physically handicapped from birth, he was a hard and intelligent worker. The youngest child, Charles Tobias or "Tobe," was just three and in addition to everything else, Muh had to watch over him.

Grandpa didn't talk much about his early life on Mayberry Creek, but it was clear that they began their new life in Mayberry with virtually no resources. The few stories he told portrayed frightening images of their desperation that first year in Mayberry, including how they nearly starved that before they were able to get a garden growing. He described how, near the end of that first summer, he and his brother George literally crawled around over the banks of the Mayberry Creek, cutting grass and weeds with a kitchen knife, trying to gather enough forage to keep their one cow alive through the coming winter. It is amazing, but they were able to cut and stack enough hay for the poor cow to survive, an essential contribution to their survival.

Grandpa also described his excitement when, not long after they arrived, he found some apple trees up the creek from the cabin, including one loaded with ripening yellow apples. Another tree nearby was loaded with sour, late-ripening, Ben Davis apples, not yet good for eating, but apples that would be good for keeping through the winter. He thought that those apple trees were truly a Godsend. He also told how dejected he felt a few days later, when he returned to gather more of the yellow apples and found they were all gone.

Details are sketchy about the family's next few years of living on Mayberry Creek, but at some point, Muh began receiving an eight-dollar-per-month Confederate widow's pension. That's a small amount of money today, but then it was enough to substantially improve the family's situation and help the boys get some education. For a period of a few years, George stayed with his uncle in Floyd in the winter months so that he could finish high school. George also attend two years at the new Virginia Agricultural and Mechanical College in Blacksburg, qualifying him for a job teaching school in Floyd.

After attending elementary school in Mayberry, Dump was somehow able to attend school at the Blue Ridge Academy in Vesta, Virginia. The school was about five miles from Mayberry, so his attendance was somewhat irregular, but he studied hard at home and appeared to have obtained a pretty good high school education. Tobe received a diploma from the same school a few years later. For many years, according to Grandpa, the boys had only one pair of overalls each. He described how, after they went to bed at night, Muh would wash their dirty overalls and dry them in front of the fireplace, so they would always have clean clothes to wear to school.

Muh, Dump, and Tobe continued to live in the little house on Mayberry Creek for almost twenty years. During that time, the cabin was improved; the lean-to was replaced with a real room and the dirt floor was covered with pine boards. A tract of about twenty acres of adjacent, more farmable land was also purchased and added to the farm that came with the cabin. While still a very young man, Dump Yeatts was known for his outstanding physical strength, and even while still in his teens, he was able to earn money by blacksmithing and by trading and training horses. He later made a mail-order purchase of a book on veterinary medicine and became the local animal "doctor."

Brother Tobe got the job of Mayberry Mail Carrier sometime around 1895, and Grandpa began serving as a substitute mail carrier for Mayberry and Meadows of Dan. While he was working as substitute mail-carrier, Dump was invited to a barn raising and dance in the adjoining community of Tobax. It was there that he was introduced to a young woman whom he been admiring from a distance for some time, occasionally glimpsing her while carrying the mail. In March of 1898, John Henry Yeatts wrote a very formal letter to Edna Rowena Reynolds in which he proposed marriage, even going so far as to suggest that sometime in August might be an appropriate time for the wedding.

Dump Yeatts was twenty-eight at the time, ten years older than the woman he hoped to make his bride, but that, apparently, was not the problem. The problem was that Edna Reynolds already had a suitor, a handsome young man named Oregon Yeatts, who was only two years older than Edna. He also happened to be Dump Yeatts's nephew and the owner of a prospering lumber business. Grandma recalled years later how the choice between the two came down to the single factor that had defined much of her life. Oregon Yeatts was not much of a drinker, but he professed no particular objections to liquor. John Henry Yeatts, on the other hand, was a sworn tee-totaler, or at least he assured Edna Reynolds that he was. Based on her childhood experiences with an alcoholic father, Edna Reynolds was not about to risk her future with a man who would even consider taking a drink. She quickly wrote back to John Henry Yeatts, accepting his proposal on the condition that the marriage date be moved up a month or two. That way, she would not have to spend all summer hoeing corn for her father.

The marriage was solemnized at the home of the bride on June 23, 1898. Grandma was an ardent Missionary Baptist and Grandpa still considered himself to be of the Church of the Brethren, but Reverend Billy Shelor, a Missionary Baptist minister from Meadows of Dan, a friend of both of them, was chosen to officiate. Grandpa and his new bride moved into the little cabin on Mayberry Creek, beginning their new life together in the two room cabin along with Muh and Tobe.

The same summer that Dump and Edna married, Dump and his brother George were able to scrape together enough money to buy "The Moore Place." Mayberry resident Aubrey Moore decided to move to Indiana, and he sold them sixty acres of land connected to the place on Mayberry Creek, and a three-room house located right beside the Mayberry Road. In December of that same year, the family suffered a terrible blow when an outbreak of measles in Floyd took George Yeatts's life.

Tobe Yeatts married Stella Barnard in 1899 and shortly afterwards bought about forty acres of land in Kettle Hollow. This land, about a mile up Mayberry Creek from Muh's little cabin, was adjacent to the land purchased by Dump and George. Tobe built his new bride a sturdy little two-room house in the Kettle Hollow, where it still is in use today.

About a year later, Dump Yeatts moved everyone; his wife Edna, their new infant son Coy, and his mother Muh, into "The Moore House" on Mayberry Road. Grandma Edna wrote in her own memoirs about how thrilled she was with the house, which was so much larger and more accessible than either the cabin on Mayberry Creek or the home in which she was raised. They had moved "right out there on the road, where they could keep up with everybody and everything going on in Mayberry."

Dump got busy with improvements to their new home right away, one of the first being the installation of a small wood-fired cooking range in the kitchen. Grandma wrote that one of the happiest days in her life was the day she got that first cook stove and no longer had to use the fireplace for cooking. The precise order in which the many eclectic additions to the house were made is not known to any living person, but by nineteen twenty-five, the house had ten rooms and two stories and presented a rather stately appearance, sitting there near the foot of a hill above the Mayberry Road.

Tobe Yeatts and his family moved to Montana in 1910, and since his brother Dump was already an experienced substitute, he took over Tobe's job as the Mayberry Mail Carrier. This opportunity greatly increased the security and well-being of my grandparent's growing family. Grandpa eventually bought the house and land that Tobe's family left behind.

"Dump" and Edna Yeatts lived in the house on The Mayberry Road from 1900 until 1967. As the family grew to eight children and the house gained its added assortment of rooms, the farm expanded as well, eventually to over two hundred acres. However, much of the land was really not very productive, and after the children were grown and the Blue Ridge Parkway had split the farm in half, Grandpa scaled back his farming and began giving away the accumulated acreage to his children.

Dump Yeatts was not one who easily shared his complaints, but he did remark that he once thought that his family's early days in Mayberry were filled with hardship. But he later realized that the pioneers moving westward suffered similar difficulties, and most experienced them daily and for a very long time. Dump was an avid reader, and he was often at odds with prevalent local political opinions. He was an early supporter of women's suffrage, and a skeptic about the righteousness of our cause in the First World War, which he thought was the disastrous result of rivalry among royal cousins. Although he lost most of his hearing and the sight in one eye when he was in his eighties, he maintained an interest in politics and world affairs, continued to read his newspaper every day. He retained a sound mind until the very end.

If Grandpa knew the financial details about the loss of the family's home on the Mayo River, he never shared them. The only thing I ever knew about his business dealings was that he never banked in Stuart (formerly Taylorsville). He did most of his banking either in Floyd, Virginia, or in Mt. Airy, North Carolina. When a bank was opened at nearby Laurel Fork, Grandpa made some small deposits there, but he continued to do most of his banking elsewhere. That was a good thing, because that Laurel Fork Bank went bankrupt in 1937 and he lost whatever money he had deposited there. Some of his neighbors lost all their savings.

By today's standards, my grandparents were far from wealthy. But they were able to educate their children and help them out by giving each of them a parcel of land. After Edna died in 1966 and John Henry died in 1967, there was little left; just enough to pay their medical bills and funeral expenses. They left this world owing money to no one, and to Grandpa, that was a very important thing.

I often think of the fantastic historical and technological changes my grandfather observed over the course of his long life. He was born only five years after the end of the Civil War and one year after the completion of the transcontinental railroad. He was six years old when Bell invented the telephone, age thirty-three when the Wright Brothers took flight, and thirty-eight when Henry Ford began building the Model-T. He was forty-two years old when the Titanic sank and forty-four when World War I began. He retired from carrying the mail at sixty-five and watched as the Blue Ridge Parkway split his farm asunder, all in the midst of the Great Depression. He was seventy-one when the United States entered the Second World War, and was eighty-one when, in spite of his objections, Grandma used her butter and egg money to buy a television set which could receive but a single channel in Mayberry.

Hard Times in Tobax
Memoir written in 1951

Edna Reynolds Yeatts

The saddest year in my memory is the year of 1890, when after two years of illness my mother was called to her heavenly reward. I was ten years old then, and I can remember clearly how the night after she was buried, I lay in bed and wept and prayed to go to wherever she was. For some reason, God did not seem to answer my prayers, and I was left to bear my grief and share the burden with my two sisters and four brothers.

To add to our sorrow, soon after our mother's death, Dad tried to find solace in drinking liquor, and soon he was staggering down the drunkard's path which so often leads to ruin. I remember him as being a good father until he took to strong drink, and even as a little girl I so hated the drink that turned him from a kind man into a cruel and harsh master.

There were five of us children left at home after the passing of my mother, since my oldest brother and sister, both children of my mother's former marriage, were living elsewhere. At the age of ten, I was left at home with two older brothers, one younger brother, and one younger sister. Many days and nights we were left at home alone and afraid.

Sometimes at night we would call out into the darkness from the upstairs window. Sometimes our Dad would answer from somewhere up on the trail, but more often than not we would hear the echo of our voices die out into the misty stillness of the Maple Swamp. If he did happen to answer us, we would begin watching, straining our eyes for our first glimpse of him to see how he was walking. If he was walking straight, we immediately felt better and our glum home would begin to take on a little bit of cheer.

I like to think now that perhaps my father's drinking may have been a blessing in disguise, for early in my life I became a bitter enemy to strong drink, resolving as a young girl that if I ever had a husband and a home that they would be sober. In later years, when I did have a husband and a home, they were much as I had planned.

After Mother took sick, we children had to learn to cook and prepare our own meals. There were many disasters and amusing incidents which attended our learning to cook for six people, and I often wonder how the young folks of today would manage under such circumstances.

We had three cooking vessels in the house; a pot for boiling water or making coffee, a pan for frying meat, and an old Dutch oven in which we made bread. We had to hunt for bark and twigs to make a fire for cooking the food, and woe be to us if we forgot to build the cooking fire. I recall that one day when I had put the bread on to bake, or at least I thought I had, and wandered off to play. One of the boys came to the door and yelled to me, "Hey Edna, come here quick. Your bread is burning up." I called back, "set it off the fire silly, set it off." When I ran into the house to save my burning bread, I found that I had forgotten to even start the fire under the oven. The boys were rolling with laughter, but I was so mad I threatened to fight them all.

Our home was built with hand-hewn logs, with the spaces between chinked with clay. It was a two story house, with the bedrooms upstairs. The spare bedroom had walls where the logs had been scraped smooth and plastered with white clay. The beds were made of the most meager materials, with straw ticks placed directly on wooden slats. The slats would often come loose, causing either the foot or the head to fall. Sometimes it was just too cold to get up and fix the bed, and we would just huddle in our discomfort until morning.

In spite of our rude way of life, we children were healthy most of the time, but one winter all of us did come down with the measles. I was running a high fever, and snow blew in under the rafters and covered the quilt under which I sweated. That was supposed to have been bad for me, but I remember how it made me feel better at the time. There was none of today's comfort and convenience, and no modern medicine or nursing care. But we looked after one another and somehow managed to survive.

In the spring of the same year we had the measles, the typhoid fever struck us so badly that the oldest boy almost died. For weeks he was delirious, sometimes trying to get up out of bed and leave home. I was acting as his nurse, making him stay in bed and just trying to keep him alive. I was trying to force him back into bed one day when he struck me, almost knocking me out, but I managed to get him back.

All of us got the fever; one by one we were struck by it, but somehow we all recovered. When the fever got me, I bedded down on the floor behind the door to be near the water. There were many feverish days that I don=t remember, and I can only credit the sheer toughness and determination for pulling us through. Sometimes the neighbors would visit us and bring us food. Of course, since the fever was catching, they didn't tarry for long.

We surely had some kind neighbors. I remember looking forward to the meal and flour giving out so that I could go the neighbors' houses to borrow some. That would also mean a trip back to repay them when we had restocked. I realize now that I was very lonely and it was a longing for a mother's love that made me enjoy the visits so much.

I can never forget a Mrs. Webb and a Mrs. Harrell that lived near us in the Tobax Community. They treated us kids so kindly and were always so considerate of us. Mrs. Webb would get me to rock her baby or fill some quilts so that she could go on with her weaving. She made lots of jeans linsey and blankets. Sometimes I can still hear the bam-bam of the loom shuttle as it flew back and forth. I loved her baby a lot, but the little fellow passed on before he was a year old. Many babies did not live through their first year in those harsh days.

Mrs. Harrell's home was always so tidy and neat and I admired her greatly for that. She was so kind to us. She would sit and smoke her clay pipe and talk with us and give us apples and chestnuts. Naturally, we considered a visit to the house a treat indeed.

We also had a kind and sweet old grandmother who would come and clean up our house and patch our clothes when she was able. She always wanted to take us to church. One time she wanted to take us to the association at Concord Primitive Baptist Church, but our shoes were a problem, being so rough and unshined, so she blackened them with shoe polish she made from lard mixed with soot from the bottom of the dinner pot. We made the trip to the association, walking about three miles each way. I have always enjoyed going to church and worshiping, and how I wish the young generation of today could enjoy going to church as I did. I wasn't in style, with my calico bonnet and my home-made shoes, but I know that God was aware of my presence and that to him the clothing was not important. We would hurry to get to Mrs. Webb's so that we could catch a ride in her ox-drawn wagon. I can remember that the oxen's names were Sam and Short. Riding in the wagon was not like riding in a fine automobile, but it took us there and brought us back safely.

We would try to get to church and back home before our dad got home so that he would not know that we went. My Brothers didn't enjoy going to church like my sister Bertie and I, but they wouldn't tell Dad that we went.

Our schooling was cut short when our mother died; we would get to go only for a few days every now and then, and lots of times I felt bitter because I could not go, when I enjoyed going so much. Even now, I believe that I might have amounted to more than I did if I could have had more education. My school books consisted of one McGuffy Speller and McGuffey's Third Reader. I studied in the boy's arithmetic book until I got to the multiplication table, and I read a few lessons in a borrowed Maurey's Geography. But I had a craving for knowledge and loved reading, so I borrowed all the books I could. I read Uncle Tom's Cabin and Pilgrim's Progress several times. I borrowed those books from a dear old uncle of ours.

Dad took the Atlanta Constitution and the local paper, the Patrick Press. How anxious we were to go to the Tobax Post Office on Thursdays to get the papers. Sometimes we'd go the home of the old doctor who lived near us and he'd give us things to read.

On days when we were feeling in good spirits, we would dream up a little entertainment. We would get the old hymn book down and sing the old songs such as There

is a Fountain Filled With Blood and The Ninety and Nine."
Sometimes we would play the old rhyming games that most
people never heard of, games that didn't use cards or
anything. Two of the games we played were William
Trimbletoe and Bag of Nits. William Trimbletoe was a
rhyming game that started out William Trimbletoe catches
hens, puts them in pens, some lay eggs and some lay none,
wire briar limber lock, three geese in a flock, one flew east
and one flew west, and one flew over the coo coo's nest. I
forget the rest, but the players were picked out one-by-one
kind of like eeney, meeney, miney moe. One of my
brothers figured out where to stand in the circle so that he
would always be the last one left standing.

Sometimes we didn't feel like singing; the boys
would be going at each other and war would be in camp,
with no one to stop it. I tried to be a mediator when the big
boys would get into a battle, but I often failed. I didn't
particularly want one or the other to win, so I would stand
and call to first one brother and then to the other for him to
come out, come out. Sometimes I would call until they
would get tickled at me and finish up laughing.

We were happy to see the big snows we would get
back then, when we would slide down the hill on planks
and old chair frames all day long. Of course, our feet
stayed wet the whole time, but then we would cut a back
log and get a fire going and get all dried out.

It wasn't too long into winter when we would start
looking forward to spring. When the first warm days
would come we'd be out to tap the maples to see if the sap
had risen yet. The big boys would tap the trees with hollow
elder tubes and we would catch the sap in cups. We
thought the sweet sap was a grand drink. One day we
gathered so much that we decided to make some maple

sugar. We had over a gallon of sap, so we took it home and began boiling it down. We boiled it until there was only about a pint left. You can imagine our disappointment when we tasted it and discovered that we had a mess of bitter half-sweet syrup that even the pigs wouldn't eat. The smoke had gotten into it and ruined our chances for maple sugar.

And as spring got near we always were thrilled by the returning of the birds and frogs. Their songs seemed to fill our green meadow with awakened hope; we would shed our old worn shoes and go tripping across the green grass, picking violets and dandelions and other wild flowers. I remember the joy of springtime and the cool tickle of the grass on the bottom of my feet, but I also remember a knocked toenail, and how the joy of springtime was knocked with it. A part of our spring festivity was hunting for birds nests. It was a contest, with the one finding the nest with the most eggs being the honored member of the brood. We had been told many times not to disturb the nests except that it did not matter for cat birds, since they got all of the berries.

On Sunday we were alone and hungry and lonesome, so when we started out to hunt birds' nests I reckon we got a little mean as well as hungry. Somehow we decided that we should gather a lot of bird eggs and cook them. We hunted on and on until we had found quite a lot of eggs, then we took them home where we scrambled and cooked the bird eggs and ate them. That night we were all sick and vomiting, and we knew that we were being paid for robbing the birds' nests.

The creek that ran near our front door was not only the scene of many happy hours of wading, but it also afforded a little meat for the table in the form of mountain and brook trout. I would often go fishing with my younger brother; he would do the fishing while I would bait the hook and clean the fish. He was really quite the fisherman, and I actually hated cleaning all the fish when he caught a lot of them, but I sure didn't mind cooking and eating them.

I don't recall that we ever had any canned food. Dried beans, shuck beans, buried cabbage and turnips were our winters' vegetables. At times we would have milk, but then Dad would up and sell the cow. Fried meat and bread are not so good without milk to wash them down.

The first cow we had, Dad had to hire a neighbor to milk it until the boys learned how. When we had a cow we would pasture it with the mules on Chestnut Hill. It was my job to drive the cow to the milking gap, but I was scared of the mules. One days the mules ran me up an old stump and kept me treed up there for half a day. Imagine my surprise and disappointment when I arrived home to find that no one had missed me yet.

These are memories I am writing for our children and grandchildren. Perhaps it is not so interesting, as the times have changed so much, but it is the way I traveled when I was a child. My husband and I have celebrated out fiftieth anniversary and we are surely facing the sunset of our lives. Our children are all married and gone, but as long as we are able to care for ourselves, life will remain grand. We had nine children and were fortunate enough to raise eight. They are all fine children and mean so much to us.

I tried to raise our children to fear God and to keep his commandments and to be sober and to never use liquor in any form. I have seen the destruction of so many lives and homes brought on by liquor. The illegal making of liquor was on every side of us, and I remember how we hated the ones from whom our Dad would buy his drink. I still have the letter I tried to write to the authorities at the county seat to get them to stop the sales of it. I couldn't write well, but I half wrote and half printed a letter which I hoped would do some good, but then I could never find the two cents with which to mail it.

My dad was a skilled shoemaker, and with the boys helping with the sewing, he could turn out several pairs in a week. Each time he would leave with several pairs to sell we were elated, hoping that he might buy us something we needed or pay up some of the debts. Usually he would be gone for days, often coming home broke and dejected with all of his money spent for drink. He always had plenty of pals when he had plenty of liquor. They would sometimes come home with him on cold nights and shake us out of bed to fix food for them. Sometimes one of the older brothers would have already found the bread I had put away for Dad when he came home, and then I would have to build a fire and cook more bread, and sometimes we kids were sent to buy more liquor. We were scared to death as we ran along the dark path through the woods with a smoky lantern to light the way.

One night when Dad came home with one of his drinking pals, all we had in the house to eat were some eggs and a nice mess of fish we had just caught and cleaned that day. When Dad told us to cook them something to eat we asked, "Which should we cook, the eggs or the fish?" His drunken friend replied, "Why cook the fish and the eggs also." We were plenty mad, but we cooked them and they ate every scrap, leaving us without a morsel of food in the house. It is because of experiences like this that there can be no kind thought in my mind for people who drink, and I sincerely hope that these experiences I have set down may help my grandchildren or some other youths to beware of strong drink. As time rolls on, drink continues to be public enemy number one in my mind.

One of the brightest spots in our lives as children was when we would get to visit our Aunt Sally. To us, a visit with her was like a visit to Yellowstone Park would be to a child today. She was a very kind and sweet old lady, and she always had lots of apples, even in the wintertime. Her house was surrounded by lilacs and roses in the spring and summer making it the most beautiful place to us. It was a long distance to her house, and we would walk fast because of our greatest fear, that of meeting a mad dog. We'd also make the journey as quick as possible to give us more time to stay at her house.

One thing we would do for entertainment was to build ivy houses. The boys would cut the tops of ivy [rhododendron] bushes and lap then together and keep building them up until we had a sunny platform to play on. We had the woods on one side and the ivy breaks on the other.

When we first moved to our house near the creek, the pheasants had a log nearby that they would drum on. Sometimes the boys would kill a pheasant, and we considered that the best of any kind of meat. There were also lots of big owls nearby, and at first we would be quite scared when they would begin their "who, who, whowhowhow-twahooo."

We had kind of adopted our Uncle Tom's dog for protection. His name was Dandy, and when we needed him, all we had to do was call, "Here Dandy, here Dandy." and he would show right up. One time, when a strange cat had whipped our own cat and chased him away from home, we set Dandy on him. What a fight that was! Dandy got the cat into a pond in the creek, but I think the cat would still have whipped Dandy if we hadn't helped out. I carried rocks for my brother to throw at the old cat until he finally gave up and ran. I thought I had done a great thing, but when we told Dad about our adventure with the cat, he told us an old saying that a wet cat will come into your bed that night and we began to doubt if we had done the right thing. But we really were right in helping out Old Dandy.

I could write on and on, but maybe these are enough glimpses to give you an idea of what my childhood was like, some days of which were very hard indeed. Sometimes Dad would declare that he was going to quit drinking, and he might stay sober for a month. When he was sober, our lives would take on a different meaning. But then he would break over again and we would despair of his ever doing anything worthwhile. He eventually married again and raised another large family, but he died homeless and pretty much alone. Of Dad's first family, there are five of us still living; the oldest is seventy four and the youngest is sixty seven. We all know that our best days are passed, but that God had been with us when we needed help the most, and I am trusting that our tomorrows will be far better than some of our yesterdays.

J.H. Yeatts in his Mail Buggy

Circa 1915

A Man for All [Trout] Seasons

Great Uncle Len, born Isaac DeLeon Reynolds, circa 1875, was doubtlessly much of the inspiration for my grandmother's life-long jihad against alcohol. Uncle Len was alleged by some to possess many of the vices attributed to the stereotypical mountain man: He made, drank, and sold illegal corn liquor, and while not too keen on hard work for himself, he demanded much of it from his wife and children. While his family struggled to keep body and soul together, his passions in life were hunting and fishing, telling tall tales, and playing the fiddle. My grandmother would sometimes use him as an example when pointing out to her grandchildren that being well-liked is not as important as being well-respected.

The first time I saw a W.C. Fields movie as a child, I thought I was watching my Great Uncle Len. Although Uncle Len was apparently a much taller man, his portliness was similar to the famous actor, and the ruddy bulbous nose and shifty eyes were identical. One characteristic Uncle Len did not share with W. C. Fields, however, was Fields's famous aversion to children. Uncle Len liked nothing better than having a bunch of nieces and nephews gathered around as a willing audience for him to entertain with funny songs, playing the fiddle, and, much to our parents' consternation, filling our heads with nonsense about the imaginary exploits of his youth.

Although Len Reynolds could claim proficiency in several professions, including veterinarian, land surveyor, and horse-trader, the two which appeared to serve him best were those of auctioneer and game warden. More than anything else, this combination of professions enabled him to work the system.

He did dabble in moonshining in his younger years, but making it was such hard work that he soon decided to concentrate on the retail end of the business. He preferred to not be involved in anything so crude as simply selling the stuff to anyone who might just walk up wanting to buy, mind you, but rather to use it as a premium in the promotion of his other endeavors. He considered himself to be a connoisseur of white lightning, if there is such a thing, and his early association with the manufacturing end of the business did give him special insight into the many factors which enhance the quality of the product. He cultivated amiable relations with those in the area who produced the finest hooch, and he was always able to make sure it was available in generous supply for his clients.

When Uncle Len was auctioneering, he was known for the strategy of providing plenty of good liquor for potential bidders. The resulting impairment of the bidders' judgments often meant that he would obtain higher than expected prices for the items being auctioned, a result which established his reputation and stimulated a demand for his services. Even folks who knew perfectly well what he was up to could not resist the enticement of such fine free liquor. Consequently, they would often find themselves the proud owners of items for which they paid a fine price and had little use.

My grandmother used to tell about how, as children living in poverty, they were often dependent on catching wild fish and game for their very survival. As a result of this necessity, Len and his siblings all became expert hunters and fishers. As an adult, because of this expertise, Len and would often serve as a guide for wealthy occasional outdoorsmen from nearby towns. The fact that he could be counted on to provide superior quality mountain dew also contributed to the demand for these services. A day of hunting or fishing in the mountain streams around Mayberry with Uncle Len as guide would usually end back at his house, with a delicious meal cooked by his dear, overworked wife, Aunt Nanny. Later, the mountain guide and his cronies would sit around the table until far into the night, drinking liquor and trying to outdo each others' tall tales. This part of life in the Len Reynolds household was described to me by members of his family many years later, and still with considerable bitterness. In all fairness, though, it was a hard time to be making a living in these mountains, and I think Uncle Len was really using whatever skills and opportunities he had available to provide for his family.

Len Reynolds's job as a game warden meant that he had special insight into the best places for hunting and fishing, and he was not above using his authority as game warden to pressure competitors to seek other fishing streams and hunting grounds. As a game warden during prohibition, he was recruited to assist Federal Agents in their campaign against the manufacture of illegal whisky in the area. He is alleged to have been especially adept at leading the Federal Agents to the distilleries of those who provided spirits for his competitors, while diverting them away from his suppliers.

By the time I knew Uncle Len, age and poor health had moderated his behavior considerably, but whenever local wags would get together and begin swapping stories about colorful local characters, some tales of Len

Reynolds's exploits were sure to come up. He was the victim in these tales about as often as he was the perpetrator, and in one of my favorites, the tables were definitely turned. It goes something like this:

A group of Stuart lawyers, all long-time clients, wanted Uncle Len to accompany them on a fishing expedition down the Dan River. He was already obligated to conduct an auction that day, but he provided them with a trusted substitute instead, inviting them to his house for libations after their day of fishing was done. When the fishermen and their substitute guide arrived at Len's cabin late that evening, he met them out on the front porch and naturally, he inquired about the success of their day of fishing.

"Hell-fire, Len," the organizer of the group, Will Joyce, complained in disgust. "It was a terrible day. We didn't catch one fish. We, didn't catch nothin' but a couple of ole' mud turtles, and of course, we just threw them back."

"Threw them back!" Len appeared aghast. "Why'd you do that? Them's some of the finest eatin' there is. I would'a loved to have fixed 'em for you. I must have cooked up a thousand."

"Well then, bring 'em out boys," Will instructed his fisher-friends.

Two of the fishermen had been standing quietly in the back of the group holding a large gunny sack, and now they carried the sack up to the cabin. They hoisted the sack up onto the porch and inverted it, dumping six big mud turtles, six large, angry, snapping "cooters," as they are called, right at his feet.

Len Reynolds was never at a loss for words. "Fellers," he announced as he danced backwards away from the scrambling and snapping turtles. "I'm the biggest damn liar in the world. I wouldn't know where to begin a-fixin' one of them things."

TREE VERSES

The Crab Apple Tree

Eunice Yeatts McAlexander

It stands atop a rocky ridge
Listing leeward from the wind.
    Nature's version of the bonsai craft.
The roots grasp tightly outcropped stones
    For anchorage, but to learn
Of dearth and drought from thinnest soil,
    The barest hope is to survive.
And still, each year the tree will flaunt
    A veil of blossoms, sweet perfumed,
Then flings its petals to the wind
    And waits, expectant for the yield.
Somehow, a scatter of its fruit holds fast
    To reach full growth; small pinkish globes
Held tightly by the twisted twigs,
    A gnome guarding treasure no one desires.

The Wild Azalea Garden

Eunice Yeatts McAlexander

There is a narrow, winding path
Beside a rocky glen,
and there a burst of glorious color,
A garden of the flame azalea
Untouched, unspoiled by human hand.
A cold spring brook
Flows down between the mossy slopes
Adding falling water's colored sound.

Among the trees, azalea
Of subtle shade and gorgeous hue
From palest yellow to red-orange grow,
With prefect clustered flower-forms.
And gangling, shrubby angled branching
Displays the bloom on slender stems.
I'm tempted to collect the blossoms,
Or dig and move some to my home.

But I do not. I long gaze at them,
Then sit a while on the mossy bank,
My bare feet resting on a stone, and
Absorb an image of the whole.
Now, when spirits fall and I grow weary,
I close my eyes, and the images I drank
Arise before me; I am renewed.
I took the azalea garden with me
And left it still untouched, unspoiled.

The Vanished Chestnut

Eunice Yeatts McAlexander

On yonder hill
A twisted silhouette against a leaden sky
With Limbs forever bare
A giant chestnut stands
A gray ghost gesturing to years gone by.

Tassels of velvet cream no more it bears,
No notched leaf nor brown-hulled nuts.
No rising spring or earthen drink stirs twigs to life again.
No more do sleek brown sprouts venture forth
In quest of sun and life and air.
The very roots are dead.

The wind in its gaunt branches moans a dirge
For fallen fellows of its kind.
No more, no more, great trees, no more
Lone remnant of a broken line.

The Medicine Man of Mayberry
(Written in 1984)

John Hassell Yeatts

There has not been a doctor residing here in Mayberry now for some sixty years, but there was a time when this community had a doctor of its very own. Actually, Mayberry had two of them at one time, but some said that one of them wasn't a real doctor. Others declared that he was too a real doctor, but whatever his certifiable professional status, one could not deny that Dr. David Robertson helped his many patients with a success rate which equaled or perhaps even exceeded that of many of his contemporary practitioners. One needs to remember that the certification requirements for Doctor Medicine were a lot different a hundred years ago than they are today, but folks were a lot tougher back then too.

His name, David Robertson, was a name worthy enough of his standing in Old Mayberry, and when he became <u>Doctor</u> David Robertson he was elevated to a position of respect even surpassing that due to his ancestral background. But his preference for walking to see his patients and often wearing overalls on his rounds soon convinced his family and his neighbors that none of his medical learning had fashioned any pretentiousness into his thinking, and everyone began calling him Dr. Dave or Dr. Davie. Sometimes his detractors referred to him as Dr. Dippy, possibly because of his short stature and his quick, erratic movements. He never weighed more than 140 pounds, and he spoke with a high pitched, excited voice that was unmistakable and seemed to carry for miles. Folks could hear him lecturing to the loafers at Mayberry Store from as far away as they could see the building.

He had his causes, and one of them was regularity. He hated "con-ste-pation," as he would emphasize it. He, like many others, believed that it was the most common source of disease, or at least the source for which treatment was most readily available. "Con-ste-pation is the main cause of appendicitis," he would declare. "And it causes all sorts of other problems as well. In really severe cases, con-ste-pation has been known to culminate in serious mental illness." (Having suffered a discomforting but temporary form of the malady a time or two myself, I wouldn't disagree but that a chronic case could drive a feller to distraction.)

In the cause of maintaining a healthful diet, he was a man far ahead of his time. While holding court around the Mayberry Store sometimes, he might use his long walking staff to point to a child eating candy and lecture him or her real good. "What are you eating that stuff for, child? Don't you know it ain't no good for you? Git yourself some raisins or some dried apples." Ceph Scott, the proprietor of the store would sort of scowl and mumble to himself. He had raisins only around Christmas time, everybody had dried apples at home, but he had lots of candy in the store all of the time. But Mr. Scott knew that on the balance, the presence of Dr. Davy holding fourth in his store was good for business.

Dr. Davie was a great proponent of eating wild greens; dandelions, creasy greens, wild mustard, and poke sallet, to name a few, each one the recommended cure for its own special list of discomforts. When the Mayberry citizens observed their friends and neighbors scratching and poking around on southern slopes in early spring, they knew that those folks probably were just following the good doctor's advice. "A mess of Creasy greens is a heap better for you than a toddy of ol' corn likker," he would say. "Either one'll keep yer blood a-tingling, but the greens won't have you feelin' bad come morning." And then he would laugh in his high-pitched cackle.

David Robertson became interested in medicine early in life, and when at school, he was found to be quite bright and highly articulate. Some of his teachers urged him to go to normal school and become a teacher himself, but David's ambitions were focused on the model of old Doctor Martin, who was then practicing medicine from an office in his big log house in Tobax. While just a teen-ager, young Davie used to love to visit and talk with Dr. Martin, wondering at the fruit jars containing preserved specimens of human organs and gazing at the grinning skeleton that stood in the corner of his office. Dr. Martin was impressed with the intelligence and sincerity of the boy, and he accepted David as his apprentice while the boy was still in his teens. David justified the confidence that the doctor had placed in him by reading and studying long and hard. During his second year as an intern, he began riding beside and sometimes aiding Dr. Martin as he visited his patients in the hills, and became what would today be described as Dr. Martin's "physician's assistant."

While he was accompanying Dr. Martin on his rounds one day, the old doctor instructed Davy on some of the finer points of medical diagnostics. "Sometimes you can learn more by just looking around the place than you can find out by examining the patient. You should always be looking for things in the patient's habits that might be contributing to his or her illness. Sometimes you might need to ask for a drink of water, but then only pretend to take a drink as you smell it. Typhoid is spread through bad water, you know."

"And above all," Dr. Martin concluded his short lecture, "never tell patients that you can't find anything wrong. Give 'em some really bad tasting medicine or tell them to do something they haven't been doing. That will make them feel better, even if their complaints all come from inside their heads." Doc Martin may have been an old country doctor, but he knew some human psychology.

At the end of the very next visit, Dr. Martin gave the patient a stern lecture about the condition of his liver, emphasizing how important it was for him to avoid consuming alcohol. As they drove away in the buggy, Dr. Martin explained to Davy how, while pretending to tie his shoe, he had looked under the bed and seen a jug which, he suspected, contained corn liquor. Then Dr. Martin announced, "Davy, I'm going to let you practice your diagnostic skills on this next patient. She's been a conundrum for me for years."

They arrived at the patient's home to find the poor lady bedridden by a litany of seemingly unconnected complaints. After a thorough examination and thoughtful inquiry, Davy told the lady that he thought that she had become too religious and his advice to her was that she should give up some of her church work. The lady was highly offended.

The two had not traveled far from that patient's home when Dr. Martin let his intern know that he was not pleased with his diagnosis. "Where on God's green earth did you come up with any such affliction as 'too religious'?" he demanded.

Davy, with a twinkle in his eye, replied. "I was just following the diagnostic method you were just describing.

While I was examining the lady back there, I bent over and pretended to tie my shoe. That's when I saw the preacher under her bed."

Dr. Martin was speechless. He looked for a moment like he might succumb to apoplexy before Davy could to explain that he was only joking. He had been unable to come up with any diagnosis other than hypochondria, but he felt like he had to tell her something. Knowing how religious the lady was, he was just inspired to diagnose her problem as "too much church work."

Dr. Martin sternly informed Davy that medical diagnoses were no joking matter. Then, with a chuckle, he told Davy, "You sure had me going there for a while." Then he added, "I guess that was about as near-on a diagnosis as I would have made."

Eventually, David took the series of written and oral examinations required by the State of Virginia for certification and was found to be worthy of the title "Doctor of Medicine," no small feat for someone who had never spent a day at a university or seen the interior of a large hospital. David continued to work with Dr. Martin until the old doctor died and he then took over the practice. He soon abandoned the use of a horse and buggy in making his house calls, though, and began visiting his patients by walking across the hills.

As he hiked, Dr. Davie would lean on a staff that extended a good six inches above his head, and the old folks said they used to marvel at how he traveled at such an incredibly fast gait. They would describe how he could jump the fences he encountered in stride, his big black bag in one hand and his walking staff in the other. It was claimed that if a boy was sent to summon Dr. Davie for a patient, he would have to run like the dickens to keep up with the good doctor after he had been found and was on his way for the visit.

In spite of his small size, he was appreciative of good food and lots of it, and as knowledge of his appetite became widespread, folks began trying to make certain he was treated to at least one good meal whenever he came calling. "Hit'll soften the bill ever' time," one long term patient was heard to advise.

Once when a delegation of local citizens were collecting funds to repair the road, Dr. Davie responded to the solicitation with, "Gentlemen, you all know that I only charge a pittance, and furthermore you know that I'm a woods and field man and rarely even use the roads." His point was cordially taken, although one man said later. "Yeah, and his woods and fields are what makes him so hard to find when you need him."

Few medical records were kept in those days, and it is now hard for even those who knew him to accurately estimate the number of lives he saved. He was adept at treating traumatic injuries; it was believed that he could probe for bullets, sew gashes, set bones, and deliver babies with the best of the town physicians. Much of Dr. Davie's medical practice was performed as an act of charity. Although he often knew that the patient had no money, he would pretend that he expected the fee to be paid. "When you can do it," he would say, but they were never presented with a bill. He would compound his own prescriptions from the many vials and boxes of nostrums he carried in his big black bag, and he would gather herbs and grub for the roots of medicinal plants that he would find along his pathway. These he would render into medicines and folk remedies when he found the time.

His propensity for talking long and loud and telling

exciting tales and impressive stories made him a welcome guest in the mountain homes, even if no sickness was there. He loved the people of Mayberry and was beloved by them. But when he was middle-aged, his wife died, and after that he seemed to no longer want to stay at home alone. One son had accidentally drowned in a mill pond in early life, and his other children were all married and had homes of their own. So Dr. Davie took to just sort of drifting from one sick family to another. Most of the homes around Mayberry at the time did not have telephones, so when emergencies occurred, runners were usually dispatched to try and locate him.

It was well known that his custom had become to remain in the home of his most recent patient until asked to leave or until called to the aid of another. He carried some spare clothing with him, but sometimes he would wash and dry his own shirts and underwear on a secluded creek bank. Often, his clothes would be washed in the patient's family's wash pot by an appreciative family member.

Folks were beginning to wonder if Dr. Davie was ever going to retire, until one day he abruptly quit his practice, declaring that he had "just sort'a given out." Well beyond the normal age of retirement, he simply gave up walking his paths over the hills of Mayberry and passed away a short time later.

Reminiscing about his late father, his son John once said, "I'll declare, warn't that Pappy a caution?" It was said with deep pride and affection, and Dr. Davie would likely have considered it to be as sincere a compliment as he was ever given.

The Old Yeatts Home in Mayberry

Vengeance is Mine

John Hassell heard the creaking stairs and the unmistakable sound of his mother's foot steps. Cringing, he pulled the covers up over his head, knowing well what was coming next. After a long week of hard work, Saturday night had been his time to really cut loose, but now he must pay the piper. Ma was now creaking up the stairs intent on convincing her wayward son that such behavior comes with a price.

"John Hassell, get up now, dear. I need for you to get ready so you can take me to church." John's mother, Miz Edna, was using her sweetest, most angelic voice.

It was only seven in the morning, for Heaven's sake, and church was not until eleven, but John Hassell's mother believed in early beginnings when there were lessons to be taught.   She had dedicated her life to protesting the evils of drinking, dancing, card playing, and debauchery in any of its many associated forms. Such dedication meant, first and foremost, that she must teach her own son the error of his ways.

She could tell, oh yes! She could always tell. The expert Mrs. Edna Yeatts could tell by the returning prodigal's footfalls on the stairs, no matter how late and no matter how quiet and careful. She could tell if there had been dancing and she could tell, possibly to the nearest dram, how much alcohol had been consumed.

This was an especially bad morning for John Hassell. Saturday night he had been down the mountain to the Patrick Springs Hotel where, not only was there dancing, but bootleg booze could be found nearby in generous supply. He had danced long into the night and partaken of more than a few nips of some extraordinarily potent brew. Now he was sorely in need of sufficient time and rest to ease the throbbing in his head and the gyrations within his stomach.

Miz Edna knew all that, and that is precisely why she aroused her son at seven a.m. to get ready for an eleven a.m. church service.

"Get up now, John Hassell, get up son. I don't want to be late."

"I'll be up in plenty of time, Ma. Just let me snooze for another half hour."

Miz Edna relented, but only temporarily.

She could have easily walked the half mile to the Mayberry Presbyterian Church, the church where her husband was a charter member and which she and other members of the family had attended for years. But a few years before, Miz Edna had decided that the preacher at the Mayberry Presbyterian Church was just too tolerant of the pursuit of worldly pleasures by some of the members. The minister at the Meadows of Dan Missionary Baptist Church, however, harbored no ambiguities about the eternal fate of those who engaged in such behavior, and it was only three more miles up the road. There is also the possibility that, as the family had prospered, she felt that the larger and more affluent Baptist Church in Meadows of Dan was more in keeping with her new status. Of course, Miz Edna would never have admitted to such feelings, even to herself, but her husband and some of the older children continued to attend the Mayberry Presbyterian Church.

John Hassell could not rest in comfort. He knew that in half an hour – precisely one half hour – his mother would indeed be back. As soon as his mother returned downstairs, he drifted into a fitful sleep, but in what seemed only an instant, he heard the stairs creaking again.

"John Hassell, get up now. You have got to get ready, and we must not be late. Get on up now, dear." Miz Edna's voice had become a shade more strident, although it was still only seven-thirty. It was clear that he was being punished.

The cycle was repeated regularly for several more half-hour intervals, until he heard his mother's final announcement, this time in a loud, complaining voice. "I'm leaving now, John Hassell, I'm walking to church. Everyone there will know how it's a shame and a disgrace that a son will not drive his old mother to church." Then, after a few moments of silence, "My rheumatism is really bothering me this morning, Son, but I'm walking to church anyway." And after a few more moments of silence, "Goodbye Son, I'm leaving for church now....walking." The front door slammed, followed by the sound of Miz Edna's footsteps across the porch, down the front steps and along the front walk. It must by now be ten-thirty. Time to get moving!

The wayward son leapt up, bent over the washbowl on the stand beside the bed, and splashed his face with cold water. Reaching into the dark wardrobe, he pulled out the first clothes he laid his hands on, dressed in about one minute, and gave his throbbing head two or three strokes with the hair brush. Then he ran out the front door of the house and down to the shed which housed the Dodge Touring Car.

The car would almost always start, eventually, but a precise and time consuming ritual was required. By the time it was running and warmed up enough to back out of the narrow shed and begin the drive up Mayberry Road,

Miz Edna had already hiked more than a half-mile up the road, past the Mayberry Store and the Presbyterian Church.

As Miz Edna walked, she knew what would happen, choreographed precisely to the minute. She really enjoyed her walk past The Mayberry Presbyterian Church, where the service had ended earlier, but a gossiping few of the congregation were still gathered. "Mornin' Miz Edny," they greeted her. "Good to see you on this fine Lord's Day." She also knew that any minute now, her errant son would come speeding past the church to gather up his saintly mother and deliver her to the Meadows of Dan Missionary Baptist Church just in time for the opening hymn. Even now she could hear the old Dodge roaring up behind her on the Mayberry Road.

As soon as Miz Edna got into the car, the dispensing of guilt began anew. "Well, you should have just let me walk to church, so you could keep on lying there, all comfortable in your bed. I would have gotten there about as soon anyway." Miz Edna's mastery of guilt inducement was legendary, to the point where even her own children sometimes referred to the beloved lady as their Baptist Jewish Mother.

Until he had retrieved his mother from the side of Mayberry Road, John Hassell had not even given a thought about how he was dressed. Now, as he took stock of his apparel, he was dismayed to find that he was wearing a bright red flannel shirt, a pair of green moleskin trousers, and muddy hunting boots.

As they pulled up beside the Meadows of Dan Baptist Church with only five minutes to spare, Miz Edna's guilt infusion began anew. " Son, you are coming inside to hear the sermon, aren't you? You will likely hear a message that you will surely need. You could use a little guidance along the path of righteousness."

"Ma, I do feel terrible about this, but just look at how I am dressed. I just threw these things on without looking. This red shirt ain't fit to wear to feed the cows." John Hassell certainly had a point there.

"Folks around here won't care a thing about how you are dressed, Son. The important thing is that you are in the house of the Lord on Sunday."

"No, Ma. I'm really not dressed for church. I'll just sit out here in the car and wait. I can hear the singing now, and you know the preacher here. I'm sure I will be able to hear the preacher too."

There was no question about that. Although he was a seminary-educated Missionary Baptist, in his delivery technique, the Good Reverend was a wind sucker of the old-time Baptist tradition. On some summer Sundays, with the doors and windows of the church standing open, even non-attendees could receive the benefits of his sermons from distances of a quarter of a mile. But whether or not he could hear the sermon was not the point. Miz Edna wanted her son inside the walls of that church, where salvation was practically guaranteed and she could observe the process of his repentance. But John Hassell sat hunched over the steering wheel, stubbornly clutching it with both hands.

"Well then, I'll just go on in alone. I'll just sit there in church and listen to the folks talking about how Edna Yeatts's son sits outside in the car, while his Christian Mother is inside worshiping the Lord. They will all know why you won't come inside. It's because you are so ashamed of your wayward living."

"Oh, for Heaven's sake, Ma, one sermon is enough. I'll go inside." John Hassell reluctantly dragged himself out of the touring car, slammed the car door in disgust, and reluctantly stalked along behind his mother toward the church door. But as they started up the church steps, he looked down at the red shirt and green trousers and felt a wave of panic. John Hassell grabbed his mother's arm and whispered hoarsely. "You go on in and sit down front. I'll sneak in when they start praying and sit in back. Maybe nobody will notice me back there."

Miz Edna figured she had exacted about all of the cooperation she was going to get from her son on this particular Sunday morning, so she nodded in agreement and marched proudly down the aisle, taking her usual seat in the next to the front row. The wayward son slipped in inconspicuously into the corner of the back bench, and not one person turned to look. "Home free," he sighed, relaxed and relieved as he slid down into the pew, adopting a slouch so pronounced that his head was barely above the level of the next pew in front of him.

The Preacher was a pretty outstanding orator for a rural Baptist Minister of the time. Highly animated, he was known for his clever anecdotes about how he had quickly quelled some budding apostasy with a well-chosen zinger from the scriptures.

The sermon today was about one of the Reverend's favorite subjects, having the announced title of *"The Eternal Hazards of Doing Well."* The scripture was taken from the book of Luke, and it concentrated on the folly of the rich man who was going to build big barns to store his abundant harvest and then kick back and take life easy. As he drew his sermon to a close, the Good Reverend injected the typical personal anecdote, in this case, the reenactment of an exchange, real or imagined, between himself and a well-to-do member of another church who was apparently reluctant to tithe. As the sermon grew more animated, the good reverend grew short of breath, causing him to revert to the wind-sucking cadence for which fundamentalist ministers have become renown. It went something like this:

"And he told me-ah, Preacher, he says-ah, The Lord has blessed me-ah. I believe he wants me to do well-ah, and I am going to invest my money and make some more-ah, like the good servant-ah in the parable of the talents-ah."

"And so I says to him-ah, oh, my brother-ah, Luke sees things different-ah. And I opened up the Holy Word-ah." At this point the Reverend, standing in front of the pulpit, held an open bible up and out toward the congregation.

"And I thereupon read to him-ah, the words of our Lord from Luke 12:18. *For it is easier for a camel-ah to pass through the eye of a needle-ah, than for a rich man to enter into the Kingdom of Heaven-ah.* And I looked him right in the eye-ah and I asked him, 'Just what do you think is meant by that'? "

As the Preacher arrived at the crux of his message, he became increasingly agitated, gesticulating with the bible in his left hand as he pointed with his right hand toward John Hassell in his red flannel shirt, sitting alone in the back pew.

"And when I said that to him-ah, I want you-all to know-ah, his face turned red-ah, his face turned as red as the shirt-ah, on that boy's back-ah. The RED SHIRT on that young feller-ah sitting right there in the back pew of this church-ah."

Obediently, every head in the congregation turned as one, and every eye in the church focused on a mortified John Hassell, sitting alone in the back pew, the color of his face now perfectly matching his red flannel shirt.

The "Tobe" Place

The Second Emigration

"Here they come! I can hear them coming now!" Three year old Vera had been assigned the task of watching for Uncle Tobe and his family coming down the lane. It was an early morning in April of 1910 when Tobias Yeatts, his wife Stella, and their five children, Roy, Foy, May, Amy, and Evy, came riding the wagon down the lane from Kettle Hollow. As she listen to the sound of the approaching wagon, Vera strained her eyes for the first glimpse of the horses emerging from the morning mist.

"Here they come! They're coming down the lane," Vera ran into the kitchen where her mother, Edna, was cleaning up from breakfast.

Edna sighed and dried her hands on her apron. "Oh Lordy, I was still hoping that Tobe and Stella would come to their senses."

"They're here Dump," Edna called to her husband. Dump Yeatts had taken the day off from carrying the mail so he could say a proper goodbye to his brother and his family, who were bound for Montana.

"I heard." Dump's terse response reflected the sadness of his entire family on this foggy morning. This was the moment they had been dreading since that evening last winter, when Tobe and Stella had announced, out of the blue, that they were selling the farm and moving Out West.

Tobe Yeatts moving his young family to Montana simply did not make sense to his brother, Dump. Tobe had a secure job as the Mayberry mail carrier, and they owned about eighty acres of pretty good farm land and their own house. Tobe and Stella had built the sturdy little two-room house the first year they were married, and it had at least kept them warm and dry for eleven years, but it was crowded now, with five children and another on the way. Dump and Edna had known for years that Tobe and Stella had been squirreling away every penny, but they just wrote it off as their frugality. Then, just last winter, they learned that the money was being saved toward the dream of owning a ranch Out West.

No question, there was limited opportunity in a mountain community such as Mayberry at the turn of the twentieth century. Many families living on the steep mountain farms around Mayberry, Virginia were now into their third or fourth generation, and all of the good farm land there had long been taken. The splitting up of family farms to be divided among the children of large families meant smaller and smaller acreages, generation upon generation. The availability of land was reaching its limit, and lots of folks in the East were moving west.

Two of Stella's older brothers had moved to northeastern Montana several years earlier, and they wrote back glowing reports of the vast tracts of fertile farm land which could be bought from the Black Foot or the Assiniboine Indians for just a few dollars an acre. One of Edna Yeatts's cousins and his family had emigrated to Montana just two years before. Edna's older sister, Flora, married to another one of Stella's brothers, had moved to Colorado. Everyone who had moved Out West reported back to Mayberry that they were far more prosperous there than they could have ever been, had they stayed back East.

Life in the Western Plains may have been rugged, but to these determined mountain people, trying to build a ranch in the untamed west was more appealing than to continue trying to wrest a living from a rocky hillside farm or, even less desirable, going to work in the stifling cotton mills of Danville, Virginia.

By the time Tobe and Stella revealed their intentions to emigrate, they had already planned their move in minute detail. But the reality that they were moving came like a bolt from the blue to Dump and Edna. Tobe and Stella were their nearest neighbors, and the two families were very close in their daily lives. For years, brothers Dump and Tobe had been helping each other with the farm work, borrowing horses, cutting wood, killing hogs, and building barns. Tobe wanted to sell everything to Dump. Though crushed by the thought of his brother leaving, Dump agreed to buy their place, and the price he paid Tobe was more than he could have gotten from anyone else.

Stella was Edna's closest friend, and for years they had depended on each other for support. Now the reality had dawned that they were going to be separated, perhaps forever. The two women helped each other daily, looking after each other's children as they shared routine tasks such as caring for their gardens and preparing and storing food for the harsh mountain winters. Just the year before, Dump and Edna's five-year-old daughter, Clarice, had suddenly become frightfully sick. Dump had ridden to get the doctor and Edna was at the child's side, tending to her when she realized that her daughter was dying. She scooped the small body up in her arms and ran screaming up the lane to Stella's house, pleading for someone to please save her child. Clarice passed away, but Stella's strong support had been indispensable to Edna's survival through her ordeal of awful grief. And now the two women were going to be separated by a distance of two thousand miles. In 1910, that seemed to Edna as though Stella and her family were moving to the dark side of the moon.

As the wagon pulled up beside the house, a forlorn and weeping family filed out through the door and down the steps to greet and say good bye to the travelers. One by one, Tobe's family climbed down from the wagon, and silently, except for the sobbing and an occasional "God bless you," everyone in the one family hugged everyone in the other. Then Tobe firmly announced that they had to get going, and one by one, they all climbed back into the wagon and they were on their way. As the horses pulled the wagon onto the Mayberry Road, Tobe called back over his shoulder, with a bit of bravado, "We'll write – let you know how we're doin'. You'll be comin' West yourselves in a few years, I'd bet." And with everyone weeping and waving, they disappeared into the mist from Mayberry Creek that still shrouded the road.

About five minutes up the road, almost to the Mayberry Store, Tobe and Stella heard a faint, breathless call, over clatter of the horses' hoofs and the creaking of the wagon.

"Wait! Please wait up." Tobe pulled back on the reins and called "whoa, whoa" to the horses, quickly bringing the wagon to a halt. Five year-old Lora came breathlessly running up beside the wagon and stretched up, handing a small rectangular object to Stella. It was a small, metal framed, tintype photograph of Edna, Dump, and the five children.

"Mama said to give you this, so you-all won't forget us." That was all that Lora said, as she turned and ran back down the road and into the mist. As Stella looked closely at the picture, her eyes filled with tears. Little Clarice was in that picture, and now she was gone. Stella wondered out loud if she would ever see any of these dear people again, and if her own family would all survive their new adventure. She opened her carpet bag and slipped the picture inside, thankfully unaware that her youngest daughter, Evy, would also be gone in less than a year. Stella also knew that she was pregnant with a sixth child, but she had not yet told Tobe, for fear he might back out of their westward move.

Tobe and Stella had planned well for their move to Montana. All the large items they were taking had already been crated up and sent ahead. The farm and the house had been sold to Dump and Edna, and most of the furniture and the livestock had been sold to other family members. Tobe already had an agreement to sell the horse and wagon to a livery stable in Christiansburg, where they would board the train to Charleston, West Virginia. If the price of land was really as low as they had been told, they had enough money to buy a thousand, maybe two thousand acres. They planned to stay with Stella's brother, Eck, while searching for just the right land to buy.

From Charleston, West Virginia, they took the train to Cincinnati, and from there, another train across Indiana and on up to Chicago. When they left Chicago, Tobe thought, they would really be heading out and into the Wild West of North America, out across Minnesota and North Dakota and into Montana. Fifty years earlier, a move from Virginia to Montana would have been by wagon all the way and would have taken about three months. But by 1910, thanks to the wonders of America's railroads, this trip was going to take only one week.

Two months after their departure, Edna received a letter from Stella telling everyone back east that they had all arrived in Montana safely. Later, Stella wrote that she and the children were in the railroad town of Saco, where they would stay over the winter. Tobe had purchased a thousand acres of land north of the Missouri River near Fort Peck, and he was out there now, building a house so they could all move out there next summer. When Edna and Dump read about the amount of land that they had purchased, they were astounded. Dump allowed that he couldn't imagine how one family could farm that much land.

For the next few years, the letters to the folks back east were few and far between, as Dump and Edna wondered and worried about how Tobe, Stella, and family were doing. Apparently, the farming and ranching efforts in Montana were not going all that well. The growing season in northern Montana was really short for corn and oats, and it was proving really difficult to plow the buffalo grass sod. Stella's brothers were apparently doing pretty well with their cattle ranching, though, as they now had over six thousand acres. That sounds like a lot of land, but in Northern Montana, that would sustain about six hundred head of cattle.

Not doing so well at ranching, Tobe purchased a well drilling rig, and was soon doing a good business drilling for water on the neighboring ranches. Then, in a story that sounds like a B-grade western movie, Tobe got into a serious altercation with a big-time cattleman. For a number of years, it seems that the cattleman had been buying up cattle from the small ranchers along a trail he had established near the Milk River, and driving the accumulated herd to the stockyards in Saco for shipment to Chicago. The land which Tobe bought had officially belonged to the Blackfoot Indians in the region, but it was range land across which the drover was accustomed to moving the cattle unimpeded, with the cattle foraging and grazing along the way. Now Tobe had fenced a part of that range.

The first year after Tobe had fenced the land, the cattleman and his drovers just cut the fence and drove the cattle through and right across Tobe's land. The next year, Tobe was waiting for the cattle drive at the fence when they arrived, and he warned the drovers to not bring the cattle across his property. When they tried to drive the cattle right through the fence, Tobe shot the cattleman who was heading the drive, though not wounding him seriously.

A couple of months later, the cattleman sent word to Tobe that he was again getting ready to drive his herd across the land, and if he laid eyes on him, Tobe would be a dead man. When the threat was reported to the local sheriff, the sheriff sided with the cattlemen, telling Tobe that he had no business fencing in that land and if Tobe got shot interfering with a cattle drive, it would be his own fault. The sheriff added that, with a great world war going on and the army needing beef, and it was downright unpatriotic to interfere with the movement of cattle across the range.

Tobe was the newcomer to the area and was on his own, while the cattleman had several ranch hands working for him. Many of the neighboring ranchers also wanted to maintain their easy access across the range to the stockyards at Saco. Almost out of money, Tobe sold the land for what little he could get, while Stella and the children moved back into town. Tobe took the train all the way to Nitro, West Virginia, where he knew he could get a good-paying job at the munitions plant. He had been in Nitro only a few months, when he caught the influenza and died. Tobe's body was shipped to Mayberry for burial, but the family was still in Montana. They could not even attend the funeral.

The only one of Tobe and Stella's children that maintained much of a connection with the folks Back East was the oldest son, Roy. He would bring his family back to Mayberry every few years to visit with his Aunt Edna and Uncle Dump, whom he always remembered with great fondness. But for all those years, Roy could never bring himself to travel the half mile trip up the lane to Kettle Hollow to visit the home place.

Roy Yeatts was ten years old when his family left Virginia, and he was twelve or thirteen years old before he officially started school. Stella taught all of her children to read and do arithmetic when they were quite young, and Tobe and Stella always encouraged the children to read. Apparently Roy was an especially bright boy: when he was nineteen, he graduated from high school and promptly married one of his teachers.

As Roy's wife, Helen, continued to teach school, Roy attended the University of Montana in Missoula, graduating in just three years. Helen was a devout Seventh Day Adventist, and Roy converted to his wife's faith. This church affiliation may have been helpful in his getting accepted to medical school at Loma Linda University in California.

Upon graduation from Medical School, Roy accepted a residency at a hospital in New Orleans, where he gained a lot of experience in the treatment of Leprosy. Helen, in the meantime, became a registered nurse. After practicing medicine in New Orleans for some years, Roy and Helen accepted a mission call to work with lepers in New Guinea. They worked as a medical team in remote regions of New Guinea for many years. When they were in their mid- seventies, the church which was sponsoring their work required that they retire.

Roy and Helen Yeatts retired to Meadows of Dan, a community near Roy's childhood home of Mayberry. Shortly after his arrival in Meadows of Dan, Roy drove to Mayberry and parked his car in front of the old house where his dear Uncle Dump and Aunt Edna had lived when he was a child. From there, he walked the half-mile pilgrimage up the lane to Kettle Hollow. There he stood, for the first time in seventy years, in front of the little two-room house in which he was born. "You know," Roy said softly, tears welling in his eyes, "I believe I must have taken the long way home."

The Maple Swamp Croquet Yard in 2010

The Mayor of Maple Swamp

Tall, silver haired, and asthmatic, Uncle "Vol," as he was known to the family, was something of an enigma to me when I was young. I was a little bit afraid of him because I had heard that he had a quick temper, so I always took care to be on my best behavior whenever we visited his home. He must have been about seventy in my earliest recollections, and was never any way but solicitous and kind toward me, asking me questions such as "Do you make good grades in school?" and "Has your daddy got you hoeing corn yet? You look strong enough."

He and Aunt Alma raised their seven children in a two-story, white clapboard farm house, built right beside the road in the section of Mayberry known as Maple Swamp. Like most mountain farm houses, the barn, granary, springhouse, and other outbuildings were located nearby. The most remarkable feature of this mountain home, however, was the croquet court in the front yard. It truly must have been the best groomed, absolutely level piece of ground in the Blue Ridge Mountains. And as soon as electric power came to Mayberry in the late forties, electric light bulbs were strung out over the court. The court immediately became the location of serious croquet duels among the neighboring men, involving matches which would sometimes extend far into the a.m. hours on summer nights. (Women were to be found on the court only on Sunday afternoons.) When the weather was good, many of the participants appeared to completely forget that they were farmers who would have to rise before dawn to milk the cows.

When I became old enough to give such matters consideration, I was puzzled by the curious contradiction in *croquet*, this classical diversion of the British Gentry, becoming such a popular pastime among these unpretentious mountain folk. Particularly since this was happening in a region where level ground was at an absolute premium.

Uncle Vol built the white farmhouse in Maple Swamp for his new bride, mostly by himself, when he was in his early twenties. Like many of the farmhouses of that day, the house was constructed on loose-laid flat-stone pillars. The location of the house was known as "Maple Swamp" for a reason, and as the foundation settled into varying depths of the soft, damp soil, the house began to sag and cant, giving the impression that it was much older than its actual age. The location of the home was less than two hundred yards from the location of the cabin where he was born. Like many early Mayberry residents, Volney Prentice Reynolds lived his entire life in essentially one location.

Some of the family used to tell stories which would lead one to believe that in his younger years, Uncle Vol could be quite profane when upset. But as he aged into middle-life, Vol made the decision to put an end to his use of such language. He also adopted a very strict attitude in the raising of his children, becoming adamant that they should never use profanity. The oldest son, Hampton, had unfortunately already picked up the habit of using some pretty strong language. Uncle Vol, intent on enforcing the new standards, told Hampton that the next time he heard him cuss, he was going to receive a thrashing. Hampton, having been the subject of his father's corporal discipline before, wanted nothing of that.

One day Vol assigned Hampton the task of plowing up a section of new ground in the Maple Swamp. Now, when a field is referred to as a "new ground," that means that it has just recently been cleared of trees and brush and is going to be cultivated for the first time. Although everything above the ground may been dug up and grubbed from the field in the establishment of a new area for cultivation, the earth beneath the surface continues to be full of roots and vines for years. Turning the earth in a new ground with a horse-drawn plow can be a formidable task.

Hampton hitched the horse to the single-moldboard turning plow and dragged it to the field, and with Uncle Vol at the edge of the field supervising, he righted the plow and began to turn the soil. Not far into the very first furrow, the plowshare became hooked on a tough, resilient locust root. Hampton was not an experienced plowman, and instead of backing up and chopping through the root before continuing, the boy urged the horse forward against the resistance of the root. When the root finally broke, it snapped back past the plow with tremendous force, whacking Hampton squarely across both shins.

Hampton released the plow handles and grabbed his smarting legs. "Oh Go-...," he began, at the same time glancing up and seeing Uncle Vol glowering at him from the edge of the field. Catching himself in mid-expletive, Hampton his ended outburst with, "..o-lee, ain't there more dang things to hurt a feller."

The local general store, officially the *Yeatts Brothers' Store*, was commonly referred to as *The Mayberry Store*, there being only one store in Mayberry at the time. This country general store was operated from the mid-thirties and through the fifties by my Uncle Coy. At some point in my early years, I learned that one of the best ways to find the real stories about what was going on in Mayberry was to hang around the store and listen to the conversations among the regulars. But I had to pretend to be paying no attention to the conversation at all.

I especially recall one story told by my oldest cousin, Coy Lee, when the gossip being shared turned to Uncle Vol's excitable nature. It seems that at one particular time, a problem of disappearing items, farm tools and such, had arisen in Mayberry. As unusual as that sort of thing was in Mayberry, it was concluded that someone was going around pilfering stuff. Nothing of any great value had been stolen, and no homes had been entered, but practical items such as harnesses and scythes and posthole diggers had begun disappearing from barns and sheds on a regular basis. Items such as these were of considerable value to these mountain farmers, and the people of Mayberry had long been accustomed to being able to leave tools and implements in the barnyard or even out in the field and find them right where they had left them upon their return. Not only that, but some residents reported hearing someone prowling around their homes and farm buildings at night. This was obviously upsetting to the entire community.

One moonless night during the peak of the problem, with everybody already kind of on edge, Uncle Vol's dog began barking and he thought that he heard someone outside. It sounded like someone prowling around in his barn or granary. Aunt Alma suggested that maybe it was a raccoon or a stray dog, but Uncle Vol was sure that it must be an intruder.

As Aunt Alma tried to calm Vol down by insisting that their dog would deter any would-be thief, Uncle Vol took his shotgun down from the pegs over the door. "I'll give the rascal a little taste of buckshot," Vol announced, as he broke down the double-barreled gun and inserted a shell into each breech. He then slipped out the back door and onto the stoop, Aunt Alma accompanying him, nervously clinging to his shirt from behind. When their dog joined them, Vol urged him to go for the culprit. Sic-em, sic-em, Vol commanded, but the dog just whimpered a bit and sat down beside the stoop.

"I just saw somebody run out of the barn and duck around to the side of the granary," declared Vol, but whomever or whatever it was, it remained completely invisible to Alma.

"I just saw somebody." insisted Vol. "Look! There he is, crouched down beside the granary. He's trying to hide behind the granary!" Aunt Alma insisted that it was dark as pitch and she could not see a thing.

"Ah Ha! There he is! Right there he is!" shouted Uncle Vol, pulling the shotgun up to his shoulder. Blam, Blam, two blasts were fired in quick succession, and as the echo of the gunshots died away, the night was filled with a prolonged resonating sound, almost like the ringing of a church bell. They strained their eyes in the darkness, but even after the smoke from the gunshots had cleared away, neither Vol nor Alma could see a sign of anyone. Vol concluded that the intruder must have fled and Alma concluded that there was never anyone there in the first place.

They both thought it better not to go out and poke around the buildings in the complete dark. It would be better to check to see what was missing in the morning. Vol turned around and pushed Alma back into the house and followed her inside.

At the first hint of daylight, Vol and Alma were up and out of bed, quickly dressing and anxious to go out and check the granary. They rushed out the back door to see if anything was missing or if the corpse of an intruder lay nearby.

But they could find nothing missing, and no sign of any intruder. They did discover, however, that there were now two large holes in Aunt Alma's big, black, cast iron wash pot she always kept inverted and stored beside the granary when it was not in use.

As Volney Reynolds aged into his seventies, much of the excitable nature for which he had been known in his younger years seemed to mellow away. A possible reason for this transition in his disposition could have been that, after suffering from asthma throughout most of his life, he at last had found some relief. It seems that he found an advertisement for a patent medicine in the *Southern Planters Almanac*. Touted as a miracle drug, the cure-all promised instant relief from the discomforts and limitations suffered by the many victims of asthma, hay fever, bronchitis, sinusitis, sciatica, lumbago, neuritis, neuralgia, hemorrhoids, and a host of other complaints. He immediately mailed in his order.

By his own admission, Uncle Vol was skeptical when the medicine first arrived in the mail. But he tried it and was immediately blessed with what he described as "the first real relief I had known in years." His praises for the product would have made a fine testimonial for advertising purposes, but the method by which the new medicine was administrated seemed rather strange to members of the family.

The medication, which really looked kind of like dried grass, came packed in a metal can, similar to a cocoa tin. The instructions on the back of the tin were explicit. "The sufferer desiring relief should use the dosage ladle provided inside the tin. Remove a rounded ladle of the medication from the tin, replace the lid, and place the contents of the ladle in the concavity of the lid. Ignite the medication in the lid with a match and fan the material until a portion of it smolders with a faint glow." The patient was then instructed to hold his or her face just a few inches above the burning medication, deeply inhale the smoke, and hold it in his or her lungs for a few seconds before exhaling. The stuff appeared to be pretty easy to ignite, but once lit, it just smoldered rather than burning with a flame, and it gave off copious billows of smoke that smelled something like wet hay burning.

Uncle Vol would stand over the smoldering pile of medication and fan the smoke into his face for ten or fifteen minutes, until it burned out. Often, if folks were in the house with him when he was using his asthma medication, they would have to leave due to the potent fumes.

The smoke seemed to make his coughing and wheezing even worse for the time that he was actually medicating, causing us all to wonder if perhaps the cure was not worse than the disease. But when he was all done, he really would soon stop coughing. Then he would sit back in his easy chair with a great sigh of relief and a glowing smile on his face. Soon everyone in Mayberry had to admit, for the first time since they had known him, Volney Reynolds seemed to be a laid-back, satisfied man. Mostly, the folks in Mayberry were just thankful that he had at last found some relief from his asthmatic affliction.

At the time, I thought the burning stuff smelled terrible and I was amazed that he could tolerate it. We all thought it was a great pity that someone would have to go through such an ordeal to obtain some relief from such a miserable chronic condition. Some years later, when I was away in college, I happened to be around when some guys in the dorm lit up what they called reefers. "Reefer," I was informed, was the hip term for a marijuana cigarette, a "joint." I had never before knowingly been around folks smoking stuff like that, but I thought I recognized the smell immediately! I could have been wrong, but what those guys were smoking smelled exactly like the smoke from Uncle Vol's asthma medication!

The awful possibility dawned on me in an instant. Had my dear old, grey haired and dignified, great uncle been inadvertently been puffing on the weed? No one could say for sure, but there are a few million folks in California who, even today, will testify to the benefits of marijuana as a medication for asthma and just about anything else you can name.

Much later, I ran across a newspaper article that confirmed my suspicions. The Federal Drug Administration had announced an injunction to force a patent medicine company to cease and desist from distributing a particular brand of patent medicine, one advertised as being especially effective as an asthma medication, through the United States Mail. The article said that the medication was being distributed by mail order through advertisements in a number of popular publications. The problem with the medication, according to the article, was that the main ingredient in the drug being distributed through the U.S. Mail was *cannabis sativa*, commonly known these days as "pot."

It should be added that there was nothing knowingly illegal in Uncle Vol's use of the medication. By any standard, there was little difference in his inhaling the smoke of his miracle medication and the millions of people who, about the same time, claimed to experience temporary relief from their multitude of ailments by dosing themselves with other patient medicines of the day such as *Peruna* and *Hadicol*. Back then, many patent medicines contained enough alcohol to make them test out at about sixty or seventy proof.

Mayberry Presbyterian Church

The Blacksmith Who Heard the Call
(Written in 1984)

John Hassell Yeatts

The community of Mayberry, Virginia, during the first half of the twentieth century, was populated by people of English, Scottish, and German ancestry, most of whom were hard-working, God-fearing, and law-abiding. But among any group of people, there will always be a minority of mean and ignorant individuals who have only contempt for institutions which strive to promote civil obedience and community spirit.

There were many who blamed the level of roughness and violence which persisted among some of the citizens of Mayberry in those days on the availability of whisky and a resulting high incidence of alcoholism. Many well-intentioned people were sure that Prohibition would be the salvation of Mayberry, and possibly the nation. But when all of the legal distilleries in the area were closed, they were more than replaced in number by illegal ones, and the illegal alcohol attracted an even larger lawless element. The use of alcohol seemed to actually increase, and it appeared to some that the dubious quality of the moonshine which became available made its drinkers even meaner and more prone to violence than the bonded stuff.

It was half of a day's ride on horseback to Stuart, the county seat, and if the law was summoned to quell some unpleasantness, by the time any officials arrived the instigators were long gone and witnesses to the event often had conveniently lost their memories. Sometimes a resident might be talked into allowing himself to be deputized and sworn in to keep the peace, but the pay for serving as a deputy was notoriously poor, and these were usually hard-working farm folk who really had little time to engage in serious routine patrol. They also had to keep in mind that, should they arrest an individual for some serious violation, they might be placing their families in danger from members of the violator's family seeking retribution. Many residents of the community resorted to carrying firearms for their own protection, with the result that there were four firearm homicides in the community in a period of less than ten years, a terrible statistic for a hamlet of fewer than three hundred souls. Mayberry, at one time, carried the unfortunate reputation of a place where a stranger did not want to be stranded after dark.

It was into this atmosphere of fear and violence that a tall and broad shouldered young man who was studying to become a Presbyterian minister came driving his Model-T Ford. He had little in the way of formal education when he first heard the call to preach, but he soon had so impressed some influential citizens with his intelligence, his sincerity, and his physical strength, that he was given the opportunity to attend Davidson College and then Union Theological Seminary. Although he was in his late twenties when he began his training, no one who met him could doubt that he was truly inspired and blessed with both abundant confidence and courage. Here was someone who, the Presbyterian Synod thought, would not be intimidated by the scofflaws and reprobates a minister might encounter in the Blue Ridge Mountains of Southern Virginia.

Many stories have been told about Robert Childress's life as a blacksmith in the years before he heard the call to preach, many relating to his outstanding physical strength. In one such tale, it was claimed that if a stubborn mule resisted being shod, Bob Childress would simply lift the mule off the ground and throw it on its back, then sit on its belly and proceed with the shoeing. It is definitely true that, on more than one occasion, some bully who thought himself to be as strong and stubborn as a mule, found himself flat on his own back when he dared to interfere with a service that Bob Childress was conducting. Here was a man who was peace-loving and who genuinely deplored violence, but who would not avoid a confrontation if he found it necessary.

Early in his ministry, a revival service he was conducting was interrupted by a group of drunken rowdies heckling him from outside an open window. Preacher Bob simply asked the congregation to open their hymnals to a song they all knew well and instructed them to all sing as loud as they could. With the singing underway, he slipped out the door, but in less than five minutes he was back. His hair was slightly mussed and his necktie askew, and many in the congregation did not even know that he had even gone outside the church. Witnesses later described how that he had placed four rowdy young mules upon their backs that night. What is even more amazing, two of those rowdies appeared, now respectful and subdued, in the revival congregation the following night.

The Childress ministry in Mayberry began in the little two-room Mayberry School building when Robert Childress was an intern under the supervision of Reverend Roy Smith from Ararat. It was not long from the beginning of his ministry until the school would be filled to capacity whenever he was preaching. He soon began bringing a folding, portable organ to the services. With some strong, young boy pumping the lever on the organ, accompaniment to the congregation's enthusiastic singing was provided by local residents such as Della Yeatts or Seena Chatam.

With the help of Miss Rosa Hopkins of the Central Academy Mission School, Reverend Bob organized a Sunday School to precede the preaching service. Miss Rosa would often arrive with her touring car filled with attractive young ladies from the academy who were recruited to assist with the lessons. This doubtlessly created an interest in Sunday School among some of the local young men who otherwise might not have been present.

Not long after the regular Sunday Services in the school house began, the teachers and students came into the schoolhouse one Monday morning to find the inside in complete shambles. The floor was littered with mud and horse manure, the desks and benches were overturned. The stove pipe had been pulled from the chimney, covering the floor with debris and soot. Some of the windows had been shot out and brass cartridge casings were left scattered about. The smaller children stood about with reddened eyes and runny noses, sobbing as they tried to comprehend the meanness that wrought the destruction of their school, while the older boys declared their intention to organize a posse and hunt the rascals down. The culprits responsible were never identified, but teachers Della Yeatts and Arzetta Smith assured all the pupils that day that school would be out for no more than a week. Mayberry may have been a poor community, but the people somehow found a little money and they donated plenty of labor. As good as their teachers' word, school began again on Monday, one week later.

Perhaps this was the event that prompted Reverend Bob to ask the congregation if they did not believe that a good community like Mayberry needed a good church building. As poor as the community of Mayberry was, his suggestion was quickly met with enthusiastic pledges of money and labor, and about one year later the Mayberry Presbyterian church was built. It is a sad bit of irony that the funeral of Mr. Cephus Scott, the local merchant who donated the land on which the church stands, was the first to be held in the new building. His is the solitary grave in the small grove of trees standing just beyond the northeast corner of the church.

After the construction of the church, the enthusiasm of the community was again tapped by Reverend Childress, when he led them to replace the ramshackle old school building with a new one. In the words of the Reverend Childress, Mayberry needed a school building where the students would not have to wear their mittens inside in the winter time and move their desks around to get away from the drips when it rained. The school system in 1926 was entirely local, with a little support from the County and none from the State or the Federal Government. Most of the money and all of the labor to build a school had to come from the community, but again the citizens of Mayberry were forthcoming. In the process of constructing the new church and the new school, it was found that when Bob Childress donned a pair of overalls and pitched in with the rest, he was a competent carpenter and painter as well as a blacksmith.

One day Rev. Childress was on a scaffold painting along with Mayberry resident Earnest Boyd. Suddenly, the poor man began spitting and coughing and gasping for air.

"What's the matter, Earnest?" inquired a concerned Rev. Bob.

"Well, I'll put it this way," replied Earnest, making a terrible face. "If I hadn't 'a had my big mouth open whilst talkin' to you, I'd of just been hit in the face with a big ol' glob of paint.

Folks could hear the preacher's laugh all the way down at the Mayberry Store, a quarter-mile away.

That laugh described the man; fun-loving and hard-working, he lived and preached a theology that was focused on love and forgiveness, a system of belief in which there was little room for recrimination and condemnation. He affected the lives of people by observing their needs and responding to them, and the people responded in kind. If a family was hungry, Reverend Childress would see that they were fed. If someone needed to see a doctor, he would either take them himself or find someone who would. One of the church members used to tell about Bob Childress finding that an elderly member of the community was no longer able to move about in her home. A few days later, the Reverend's little Model-T Roadster was seen bouncing up the lane to the her house, a wheelchair tied on the back.

Each Christmas, Reverend Childress would see that a tree was set up in the church, a nativity pageant organized, and gifts and treats distributed to all the children. One year, a congregation member bragged, the Christmas Pageant was so elaborate, it required the use of every bathrobe in Mayberry.

After Mayberry, Reverend Childress expanded his ministry into other communities: Slate Mountain, Buffalo Mountain, Dinwittie, and Bluemont, building Presbyterian Churches, and sometimes building schools. But when he shifted his focus on to other communities, those from which he moved from were not forgotten. He would always come back for services and meetings with the congregation. He never forgot the people and their needs.

Today, in looking back with my youthful association with the Reverend Childress and my own career and travels, I often make comparisons of my memories of him to other outstanding individuals I have met. The nature of my profession is such that, on occasion, I have been in close contact with many celebrities and persons of note, as well as a host of kind and gentle everyday working people. No one stands taller in my respect and esteem than Robert W. Childress. As I watched him change so many lives, while shunning personal stature and financial gain, even a skeptic such as I became convinced of how religious faith, taught with love and forgiveness, rather than the threat of damnation and eternal punishment, can perform miracles. In my view, his preaching and teaching were as close to the teachings of Jesus Christ as those of any man I have ever heard.

His son and namesake, Robert Jr. today serves three of the churches his father founded, including Mayberry Presbyterian Church. And to hear him expound the same religious philosophy of love and forgiveness is to me still, a beacon of light shining across black and stormy waters. Mayberry, in particular, has been blessed by the man who gave up the hammer and anvil to follow Jesus of Nazareth.

Note: Robert W. Childress Senior passed away in 1959, and his son Robert Jr. died in 2001. At this writing in 2011, Stewart Childress, the son of Robert Childress Jr., is the pastor of Mayberry and Bluemont Presbyterian Churches. The Mayberry Presbyterian Church has been led by a pastor with the name of Childress for sixty-nine of its eighty-six years of existence.

Our Suck-Egg Dog

Fred Yeatts

The architecture of rural homes in the Southern Appalachians changed dramatically in the years following the Civil War. Sawmills, powered first by water, then by steam, and eventually by the internal combustion engine, made sawn lumber affordable for new home construction. About the same time, America's new steel industry was also making nails and other hardware generally available. Not only were the new "stick-built" board houses more flexible in design and faster to build, they were considered more fashionable than the log houses, with their tiny windows and red mud chinking.

The sawn-board construction of the time was relatively easy to build wherever the owner felt suitable, without the need for excavation for a foundation or level ground. The ground-level support for the house might be simply flat rocks or posts or some combination of them, possibly even including stumps. A sloping site was often selected, with the back of the house at ground level and wooden steps leading up to an elevated porch in the front and the sloping space under the house left open. This style of construction provided several practical advantages. The ground water drained away from the house, making it less damp and moldy than a log home, and the air circulating under the house made it cooler in the hot summer months. Unfortunately, the circulating air made the house cooler in the winter months as well.

One particular advantage of the board house on a slope was the shelter it provided underneath for the several dogs which typically were owned by many Southern Appalachian families, and for their truly original, non-caged, farm-bred, free-range, pharmaceutical-free, organically fed chickens.

Only a generation or two ago, many houses on farms (and sometimes even in small towns) would have dogs lying under them, in among a small flock of chickens, the dogs sleeping while the chickens were busy fluffing up the dirt to smother their mites. The dogs and the chickens shared the responsibility for the disposal of table scraps, with the dogs providing trusty twenty-four/seven sentry duty, and the chickens providing their litter. Chicken manure mixed with wood ashes was often the only fertilizer available for rural population's organic gardens. Another plus of this arrangement was the energetic, pre-dawn crowing of the roosters providing a reliable wake-up call for the household, every day of the year.

The dogs, usually hounds, really helped the relatively poor rural population hunt the small game that provided important supplemental protein in their diets. The edible small game consisted primarily of rabbits, squirrels, partridges, and wood grouse. Occasionally, groundhogs and opossums were also eaten, if not exactly enjoyed.

For rural folk in the South, the chickens and dogs formed a synergistic relationship, the dogs keeping the ever-present foxes, raccoons, skunks, opossums, and weasels away from the chickens. From the time they first bonded, humans and dogs have shared the pestilence of the flea, as both man and dog normally return to their bed or den nightly, where the fleas can lay their eggs to sustain their reproductive cycle. Other primates, such as chimps and gorillas, although hairy, groom one another and change their bed sites nightly thereby avoiding flea or tick colonization. But the chickens with their keen eyesight and rapid reflexes, quickly eat any insect or insect eggs, limiting the infestation of fleas, ticks, other insects, around these homes. The eradication of ticks by poultry was of immense value to the health of the human population by limiting many devastating tick-borne diseases.

The hunting dogs kept around a rural home made another economic contribution back in the years when the fur from varmints was commercially valuable. When any small wild animals were caught or killed, their skins were stretched over a tapered board and dried. They were later mailed, via the U. S. Postal System, to a company such as I. J. Fox Furriers. I. J. Fox, headquartered in Pittsburg, Pennsylvania, paid fairly and timely, the value of the pelt depending upon the species and the quality. Around 1940, a good fox pelt could bring as much as eight dollars, while a good opossum fur might bring two. Regrettably, in 1948, I. J. Fox quit accepting pelts and there was no alternative furrier.

While chickens were important to southern households as a direct source of food, the trading of eggs was also important. Eggs were traded for essential household basics such as matches, salt, baking soda, sugar, coffee, needles and thread, and lamp oil. Often included were some additional, not-so-essential items, such as dipping snuff, plug chewing tobacco and patent medicines. The patent medicine concoctions, with their "patented secret ingredients," were mostly colored water and a high percent of alcohol, and they were always guaranteed to cure all complaints what-so-ever, real or imagined. The value of eggs in those days was surprisingly high by current standards, sometimes attaining a retail price of sixty or seventy cents per dozen. There developed a wide network, with the old country stores used as collection centers, for the transport of eggs, chickens, and other commodities from the rural areas of production to the markets of larger towns and cities. The management of the "egg money" derived from tending the chickens gave the women of the rural household some measure of self-esteem and independence.

The practice of chicken husbandry led to the development of that ubiquitous southern dish – spring-fried chicken – a wonderful warm-weather respite from salty ham and canned beef of winter. For my family, an important part of a "Sunday chicken dinner" was the ritual pulling of the wishbone, usually referred to as the "pulley bone." Normally, the wishbone went to the youngster who was closest to the portion of the chicken that contained the wishbone when it was served. This child and the next nearest child shared the pulling, but the issue of who was to be awarded the wish derived from the wishbone was variable, depending on the agreement as to who got the short bone or the long when it pulled apart. Because of the lack of clear agreement, this event often ended in dispute. Since one could not reveal the contents of the wish or the wish would be invalidated, the winning of the wishbone pull was not so valuable, even for bragging rights. Any cooked chicken remains from meals including splintered wishbones were fed to the dogs. These non-pedigreed dogs loved those bones and they helped nourish the dogs as part of this complementary relationship. The idea that cooked chicken bones can be fatal for dogs must surely be an urban myth, at least as it applied to hounds like those we owned in my youth.

Although the South of my childhood had often been alluded to in literature as "the place where time stood still" there had been no reported saber tooth tiger or pterodactyl raids in living memory (or attacks by bears or mountain lions, for that matter). The airborne raids by chicken hawks and twilight raids by owls, however, were a constant threat to the poultry. The small bantams and young chicks ("biddies" as Southerners fondly called these fuzzy little creatures) were vulnerable prey for these feathered predators. Our hound dogs would only raise their heads from between their front paws to observe the commotion from the alarmed cackling of all the fowl – chickens, turkeys, and guineas – whenever the chicken hawks were sailing about ready to swoop in for their meals. The dogs soon lost interest in the attacks, but the poultry all ran for cover, under the house, under porches, and under bushes. Our huge blue-grey barred Dominiquer rooster would carefully tilt his head (chickens have monocular vision), to observe the circling chicken hawks. Then he would majestically stride for the air raid shelter under the porch without bowing his proud neck, although he really had nothing to fear, as hawks or owls only attack poultry of a size that they can transport. That old rooster just didn't want to lose sight of the hens.

Each morning when we opened the chicken house doors, the chickens always rushed to exit, flapping and flying, running like kids when released from a confined classroom for recess. We usually checked carefully to find if any varmints had killed chickens. Weasels and minks were fierce poultry predators that could often penetrate the defenses offered by the dogs. Minks were destructive, but they stayed close to streams, so weasels were the real menace. Weasels are so thin and nimble that they can enter a henhouse through any crack more than an inch and a half wide. Once they are in a confined space with the poultry, they kill everything they can reach, quickly and furiously, by slashing their prey's throats. Animal specialists speculate that the hunting and killing function in the weasel's brain is decoupled from the hunger function. The popular characterization of the weasel is that of a creature which is deceptive, evasive, and manipulative. The small weasel's evasiveness is only, at most, an auxiliary attribute. They simply move on quickly after their slaughter, having no purpose in lingering at the killing ground. They don't deceive or manipulate; they just slaughter! Ounce for ounce, they are perhaps the animal kingdoms most fierce killers, proportionally even more deadly than wolverines or shrews.

My younger sister, Gerry, remembers vividly one morning when we found that a weasel had slaughtered thirteen chickens which, for some reason, had roosted in an old wood shingled shed adjacent to our granary instead of the chicken house. And once, as we walked along the dirt road adjacent to our nearest neighbor's farmyard, the neighbor called my brothers and me to view a horrific chicken slaughter executed by a weasel, possibly two. She had laid out thirty-eight dead young laying hens in two adjacent rows. She was crying bitterly as she showed us the torn throats. Not one chicken had been even partially eaten! Her chicken house was well built but she had left a small window slightly cracked, leaving a minuscule opening through which the weasel had slithered.

Early one thickly foggy autumn morning when I was a teenager, I rode with my father in his pickup truck to a more distant part of our farm to feed cattle. The dirt lane entrance to the field was bounded on the upper side by a high bushy bank and on the lower side by a small bank that was bordered in turn by a blackberry brier patch. As we turned onto the lane, we observed the perplexing sight of a limp, dead rabbit being mysteriously propelled across the dirt path. As my father braked the pickup to a stop, I absolutely could not fathom what forces were causing the rabbit to be moved. Then my father told me, "It's a damned weasel dragging its kill. Fetch me the pistol." Then I could see the little brown weasel, its back arched as it bounced over from the lower bank to the rabbit, dragged it a couple of feet, and then ran back to the bank, scouting out possible routes along which to move its prey. I handed my father the long-barreled twenty-two caliber revolver which he always had, loaded and handy, in the pickup truck glove pocket.

He carefully opened the pickup door, rested the pistol on the doorframe and firing a single shot, killed the weasel from a distance approaching forty yards. It was a remarkable shot, with the bullet hitting the tiny weasel in the neck, severing its spinal cord and killing it instantly. Holding up the tiny animal by its black-tipped foot-long tail, he showed me its lemon colored underbelly contrasting with the beautiful sleek brown and back fur. The weasel was no bigger around and only a bit longer than a chipmunk, and it must have weighed less than half of a pound. The dead rabbit, which had bled to death from having its throat gashed, probably weighed close to three pounds. Pa observed, "If weasels were the size of tomcats, they would be pulling deer carcasses instead of rabbits."

Among the problems that might arise from keeping a large pack of dogs, especially hounds, around one's dwelling, one seemed to result from their regression to some primitive form of competition, causing them to behave viscously toward strangers and sometimes even to household members. Some of my earliest memories are of one of our dogs, an old Buzzard Wing hunting hound, named Pluto. (This colorful breed was given its name for the large, prominent black saddle coat coloration on their backs which contrasted with their mostly white and tan coats. Our mother would sometimes give my younger sister and me a buttered biscuit or a cornbread crust and then shoo us out to the front porch to get us out from underfoot and to keep us from dropping crumbs on the kitchen floor. Like that sinister creature from the underworld, old Pluto would immediately spring out from under the front porch, using his wicked, deep growling to try and frighten us into dropping bread. That failing, sometimes Pluto would simply knock us down and take our bread, leaving us feeling like he could have also taken our hands in his hungry haste.

Perhaps in some stroke of cosmic justice, while he was hunting with a neighbor late one autumn day, Pluto fell stone dead while in full pursuit of a rabbit. My older siblings and parents claimed to have been saddened by the loss of this legendary tracker, but my younger sister, Virginia, and I mostly felt a strong sense of relief from the demise of the sinister old blackmailer and bread thief.

People who have a pet or two sometimes think they understand how dogs behave, but unless one has dealt with a large assemblage of dogs, it's hard to grasp the full range of threats which can be presented by their pack behavior. A few years after he returned from WWII, for example, my oldest brother who was then a rural mail carrier, was harassed by a pack of vicious hounds who would actually attempt to bite his arm as he placed the mail into mailboxes from the window of his car. One day, as he drove over the muddy rural road through one deep hollow, six multicolored coon hounds bounded from under the nearest house in full-throated attack. Simultaneously, from under the neighbor's house on the upper side of the road four large and belligerent Redbone Hounds came out bellowing and grabbing for his tires and lunging for his arm, and one of the dogs actually snagged his sleeve and bit his left hand. When he complained to the dogs' owners, the reply was always that they were "good dogs," and he had better just leave them alone.   Although blessed with a quiet disposition, he determined that the time had come to do something serious to deter the dogs from attacking him during his mail delivery.

He and his good friend, Gene, carefully plotted their response to the dog problem. Just before they drove his 1937 Chevrolet coupe down into the hollow with the dogs, they tied two empty burlap feed sacks tightly to the wooden spokes of the rear wheels. Then they raced the old coupe down through the deep red-mud ruts of the road through the hollow. The hounds all attacked in force, biting viscously into the burlap sacks as they were being whirled around by the car's rear wheels. My brother and his friend greatly enjoyed describing described the results; dogs flying through the air and hounds slammed into the mud, as the dogs' teeth would become snagged in the strong fiber mesh of the burlap sacks. They declared all the spotted hounds to have become "Red Half-Broken Bone Hounds" from the muddy, red mud coatings they received. My brother circled the car around and drove back through the hollow receiving only some distant barks from these now bruised, limping, and almost toothless hounds. From then on, these hounds remained a respectable distance from the old coupe as he delivered the mail.

There is a serious problem which can result from the close proximity of hounds and hens. Many breeds of chickens such as the Bantams and Domineckers

(Dominiquers actually, as I learned much later in life), with their rose combs and broody behavior, are naturally opportunistic creatures. Given the freedom to do so, they regress quickly to their jungle fowl practices of hiding their nests in bushes, under logs, in patches of tall grass, and often unexpected places. The perpetually hungry hounds were instinctive hunters and naturally would begin to suck any hen's eggs they would find nearby. The hounds' behavior would then progress to their actively hunting hens' nests and eventually to raiding henhouses, devouring any and all eggs they could find. The hounds' addiction to sucking eggs would lead to a downward spiral in their behavior to where the suck-egg dogs then would raid out neighbors' henhouses in search of eggs. This had the obvious potential of causing serious disagreements between neighboring households, disputes which would occasionally escalate into long-term feuds between formerly good neighbors.

When confronted, suck-egg dogs instinctively knew that they had betrayed the trust of the household and in an attempt at recompense, would whine and grovel in a most craven manner. The offending dog would often tuck its tail under its belly and drop to the ground, cringing and whining, as though begging for forgiveness. (Politicians often mimic this behavior when caught in compromising situations.) There seemed to be no known cure for the suck-egg dog addiction! Hot peppers, sulfur, and other odious materials placed in decoy eggs for these dogs, appeared to do little to discourage the addiction. The dogs could obviously smell the difference between good eggs and decoy eggs, and they didn't waste much time before moving back to devouring the good eggs. The only solution was to either keep the dog chained, which wasn't normally acceptable, as they would drive everyone to distraction from their barking, or trade them to someone on a far, far distant location and hope they'd never return.

Due to the intrinsically "sneaky" nature of the crime, and the craven and cowardly nature of the dog's behavior when confronted, the term "suck-egg dog" became the vilest insult that Southerners could hurl at an opponent during a quarrel. Even the mildest little schoolboy, in a dispute over a game of marbles or tag, could be stirred to a raging fury, should his adversary call him a "Suck-Egg Dog". The antagonist could describe in detail his lack of honesty, his deep stupidity, his incredible ugliness, his lack of personal cleanliness, and impugn his family's sexual proclivities, but these insults were comparably insignificant. But if ever the quarrels escalated to the final and deepest insult of "Why, you low-down little suck-egg dog," there would quickly be blows exchanged and tears flowing.

Our family liked dogs and found them quite useful. A special favorite was a southern type of predominately reddish, longhaired multicolored shepherd dog a breed similar to, but bigger and more burly than the Border Collie. One such dog we owned was named *Moscow* by my father, in honor of the first great defeat of the German armies by the Russians in 1941. He was a wonderful livestock-herding dog but he had a strange behavioral quirk. Whenever he found a woodland box terrapin, Moscow would become fixated, perhaps as a result of his extremely sensitive and obsessive herding instincts. He would bark at the little terrapin until the terrapin closed his shell tightly. Moscow would remain by the terrapin day and night barking sharply whenever the small terrapin tried tentatively to venture forth. Moscow always seemed relieved, as must have been the terrapin, when we found him in the surrounding woods, tired and hoarse from his siege, and led him home.

Moscow tirelessly patrolled his farm and woodland territory, one consequence of which being that often in the summer nights he would encounter skunks which he frantically attempted to drive away. Often, he received skunk spray in a full-dosage that completely saturated his beautiful long coat of hair. When we would head out in the early morning to milk our cows, Moscow's delighted rush to rub against our legs in a display of affection for his masters would cause my brothers and me to scramble for the barn. He paid little heed to our repeated shouts of "Git, Moscow! Git, you stinking rascal!"

Later in his life, Moscow became a philanderer and would disappear for weeks while looking for an accepting female collie or some other longhaired companionship, completely disdaining the homely hounds we kept at home. But back then, no one ever considered having a dog neutered or spayed.

The replacement hound for our defunct Pluto was a beautiful, well-behaved, Black and Tan that my family named *Dover* rather than the usual *Rover*. But he was only a mediocre hunter, refusing initially to hunt 'possums and often being out maneuvered by the quick cottontails, so our family continued to have space available for an additional good hunting hound.

One wintry evening a few days before Christmas, as we were feeding cattle, my older brother, Jimmy, made the statement to me that it was going to snow, either tomorrow or the next day. Although he was almost clairvoyant in predicting the weather, especially snow, I made a rash bet against his prediction. Then, I foolishly added the additional statement that, since the sky was so clear, new snow made no more sense to me than if his favorite milk cow, "Boneyparts," had twin calves, or if one of our dogs had a puppy. I told him I would bet him a dime that it wouldn't snow as he predicted, nor would either of the other improbable events come to pass. Although I hoped he was correct about the snow, I felt, with the extreme conditions that I had stated, I certainly would never have to pay, and Jimmy would soon forget the condition I had asserted regarding the birth of the twin calves. Since Boneyparts wasn't due to calve until spring, and all our dogs were male, Jimmy was probably thinking only of his bet on his snow forecast when he smilingly accepted my high stakes wager. But the following spring, Boneyparts did indeed give birth to beautiful twin Guernsey calves. I was indeed awestruck by Jimmy's winning bet, and he was delighted when I paid him the dime that I had accumulated from selling "creek-found" duck eggs.

The night following my brother's prediction, a few inches of snow actually fell and the snowfall continued into the next morning. After milking the cattle and slopping the pigs, as we came back to our house in the dim early morning light, and we were walking onto the back porch, stomping the snow from off our shoes, we simultaneously saw the beautiful little hound. She had a very light, beautifully colored blue coat, with little scattered black spots, and a white tail which hung down a bit from the horizontal. Her feet were brownish, perfectly matching the unusually long, velvety, rusty colored ears, ears which she would often perk-up intelligently. She greeted us eagerly, but not too profusely, conducting herself in a well-behaved manner. Jimmy asked me to go get an old bowl from Mother, as he wanted to give this hungry dog some fresh milk. I fetched a bowl and Jimmy fed her one pint, and then another pint when he saw how starved she was. She settled down contentedly as we looked around to see which direction she came from. But we could see no tracks in the snow.

My father was lying on his bed seeking some relief from his chronic spine disability when I asked him to come look at the hound. He slowly and painfully pulled on his overalls and shoes and walked out to examine the hound. "She's a beautiful half-grown Blue Tick Gyp," he informed us. "They are one of the best hunting dogs there is; they tree coons and possums especially good. She must have been out hunting and got lost. I'll hear of it at the store if anyone is looking for her."

My father, although nearly disabled with lower back problems, operated the Mayberry Store in addition to overseeing our farm. If anyone around had lost a dog, word of it would soon reach the store. But no one claimed the little Blue Tick Gyp and she rapidly grew into a beautiful specimen of her breed. She was of wonderful muscular trim with a long pointed tricolor muzzle and was only about twenty inches high at maturity. The Blue Tick Gyp was a fast runner with a wonderfully keen nose and exceptional night vision; in short, she came equipped to be an excellent huntress. She always led any pack with which she was hunting, and even old Dover was transformed into an effective hunting hound when he followed her lead.

When my older brothers, Charles, Jim and I went out to hunt in the late autumn evenings we carried an old kerosene lantern and a flashlight (if we had working batteries), and a burlap gunny sack to carry back any captured prey. We boys still had good night vision, as we did not yet have bright electric lights in our home. Candles and kerosene lighted our nights in those days.

As we would hurry through the thick woodlands, we always had complete confidence that the Blue Tick Gyp would "tree" an opossum or chase a rabbit in some underground den or hollow tree. She appeared to undergo a transformation into a super huntress when we would start the hunt, raising her tail high as she ran in ever-widening circles, casting about for the fresh trail of prey. When she struck an acceptable trail she would begin barking every few seconds in a very measured cadence, her unmistakable signal she was "on the hunt". Her clear bell-toned voice resounded through the hollows and over the hills as we rushed to follow her. It was pure excitement for us, listening to her from some high hilltop as she and the other hounds barked out their individual songs while pursuing their prey.

When the hounds treed their quarry the Blue Tick Gyp's bark would quicken to a deeper prolonged barking while doubling the cadence of her "treeing" bark with respect to her "on the trail" voice. We never actually caught that many possums or rabbits during these hunts, but it truly was the "thrill of the hunt" for us that spurred us on, through thickets and swamps.

Possums would usually scurry so high up into a tall tree that we would have a hard time dislodging them. I recall one particular bright, moonlight night when the dogs summoned my two older brothers and me to a large old shagbark hickory high on steep ridge. We could see a huge possum in the branches, the light from our flashlight reflecting eerily in his eyes in the dark night. My brother Charles and I lifted Jimmy high so he could grasp the first branches and climb to dislodge the possum. He climbed and climbed, finally reaching the branch where the possum was lodged. The possum was sitting out about three feet on a large solitary limb, but Jim had no stick and he was unable to tear a branch from off the tough hickory tree to dislodge him. As Jimmy approached the animal, the big possum showed his sharp, saliva-covered teeth, looking like the devil himself in the light of the flashlight from the ground below. We could hear him hissing at Jimmy's foot as he dismissed Jimmy's efforts to reach out and kick him loose. Charles called to Jimmy to use his belt and strike the possum with the buckle. Jimmy swung vigorously at the possum with his belt until he dropped it, and then threw his shoes at the creature. The possum only curled his tail tightly around the branch and further ensconced himself onto the limb, where he remained, safely surviving for a chase on some other occasion, while Jimmy had to carefully and slowly make his way back down the tree, without the benefit of his belt or shoes.

The little Blue Tick gave birth to three fine hunting hounds the following year. Her pretty and quick little white-footed black and tan pup was sold first. Then her spotted black and white hound was sold soon after that. The third hound, the best tracker, was a little white male with small black spots. He was bartered for a Syracuse turning plow, one so large that it required two strong horses to pull it, plus a carved hickory yoke for a big steer. My father said in his old age that he should have concentrated more on the hound business, as there was greater enjoyment and more money to be made in raising hunting dogs than in farming.

Our family always kept a variety of poultry such as turkeys, geese, and guineas and of course, lots of chickens. As had been the case for centuries in English country households, the oversight and management of poultry was the domain of the woman of the house, but our mother's increasing debilitation from rheumatoid arthritis meant that we children became her legs and arms in caring for the poultry. The first serious responsibilities I was assigned while still a pre-schooler were letting the chickens out in the mornings after the frost or dew diminished, feeding them, and collecting the eggs. I was proud when I was entrusted with my father's good hammer, which I used to beat broken plates and saucers and chipped cups into small bits. This task was conducted on a large white quartz rock near the hen house, where the chickens would crowd around me to gather each ceramic bit for their gizzards to grind up food in their craws.

We kids were given the additional challenging job of locating our turkeys and guineas nests in the springtime. (I accumulated seniority as a pre-school kid, since having been born late in the calendar year, state law prevented me from attending school until I was almost seven.) The turkeys and guineas ranged freely, foraging over large areas of pasture and mixed woodlands, and being half wild creatures, they naturally choose to nest in secluded areas. The turkey hens carefully covered their nests with old leaves, camouflaging them so well that they were almost impossible to locate. My mother had us keep the turkeys locked in their nightly roost they shared in the hen house until after noontime so that the laying turkeys would go directly to their nests. Her theory was good, but those turkey hens could easily elude our most diligent tracking. For all my many watchful days, I can remember only one or two occasions on which I located a turkey nest by this method. One of our turkey hens would wander to a hill some distance from our house, then suddenly sprint like a miniature airplane taking-off, then fly a couple of hundred yards over a fence into a black, muddy, swampy thicket.

My younger sister, Virginia, and I observed this on several occasions, but we were never able to find her nest. Then the turkey hen completely disappeared for over a month, until one day in June when, to our delight, she showed up proudly at the granary where we fed the poultry, her eight shy young poults in tow.

Guineas nests were easier to find, as the guinea hens would announce the laying of each egg with their loud, forty five second, zinging staccato cry of "kau, kau, kau kau, kau, kau-u," that decreased rapidly in amplitude and became quite lower in frequency with time. The guineas would lay sometimes more than three dozen eggs in a nest before attempting to hatch them. My mother, although normally not superstitious, was convinced that the persnickety guineas could smell whether a human hand went in their nest and would quickly abandon laying their eggs there. She always instructed us to use her long-handled soup ladle to avoid this problem when we collected guinea eggs, and it worked just fine.

It was most interesting to observe a little guinea hen spread her wings using every one of her feathers to cover her eggs when she began to sit on her eggs. Surprisingly, the guineas would sometimes hatch more than a couple a dozen little keets (as young guineas are called) from those huge clutches of eggs. Unfortunately, the hyper-energetic guinea hens and the long legged turkey hens would force march their newly hatched babies for long distances as they foraged for food, sometimes through the grasses wet from rain and heavy dew. Because of this, the mortality rate was high for the newly hatched fowls. We would say that they were "drabbled" to death, but it may be that the guineas and turkeys were just highly susceptible to some of the diseases harbored by our flock of chickens.

Once, when I was a second grader and my mother decided she wanted to increase our flock of chickens, I was allowed to trade three white rabbits for five silver-laced bantam hens and one bantam rooster. A friend gave me a second rooster the following spring, a gorgeous red jungle fowl bantam, and our chicken flock did indeed increase. The "Banty" and the "Shanghai Buzzard Necks"(a bald-necked, hardy, and very ugly breed of chicken), quickly out propagated the other assorted types in our flock and monopolized the barnyard, roosting at all sorts of odd places. The dogs however, were able to keep the chickens safe from foxes, possums, skunks, and the occasional prowling raccoon, all animals that specialized in capturing roosting chickens.

In August of the next year, my mother became alarmed when there were no longer eggs to be found in the lower henhouse. I began to notice that, in the afternoons after school, she was cool toward me and terse in our conversations. When I finally asked what was wrong, she dropped the seriousness of her concern on me. "Freddy," she pleaded. "Now please tell me, have you been taking those eggs from the lower henhouse and trading them for candy?" I cried and answered truthfully that I had been doing no such thing. Although I did confess to one time having taken three banty eggs from the barn and two duck eggs that Jimmy and I found in the creek and trading them for chocolate drops at the store, I swore to having never pilfered eggs from our hen house. Still, she seemed to be not quite satisfied that I was telling the truth. It's a terrible, terrible feeling to have your own Mother doubt you. (Actually, I did omit telling her that Jimmy and I had once bartered three other duck eggs to a neighboring country store for a small pouch of loose Bull Durham smoking tobacco and a package of roll-your-own cigarette papers. In addition to making my head swim, it was those roll-your-own cigarettes that stunted my growth, according to my much taller other brother, Charles. At any rate, I felt just awful and promised her that I would never trade any banty eggs without her permission.

About three days later, when Jimmy and I came home from school and started out to do the evening milking and pig feeding, our mother told us that she had seen the Blue Tick slip into the henhouse at about two o'clock that afternoon and then again about five, and Mama said she could see the hound carrying out an egg in her mouth on the last trip. The Blue Tick hound approached the henhouse from the wooded area to the rear of the henhouse to avoid detection and quickly slipped inside, finishing her devastating egg raid in only a couple of minutes. Then the Blue Tick departed cleverly the same way, slipping around quickly to the back of the hen's house and then making tracks for the woods, carefully keeping out of sight. My Mother told us directly, "I was worried that you boys might be doing something with the eggs that you shouldn't have, but I really didn't believe that you were." I felt vindicated and I was really happy to be rid of the terrible burden of my mother's suspicion, but having a traitorous suck-egg dog that had to be expelled from our household saddened us all. It was almost as if a family member had committed a terrible crime, and my father seemed the most disappointed of all.

A few days later, however, the Blue Tick was sold to noted coon hunter Jerry Puckett, who lived deep in a hollow several miles away. My father warned him that he was buying a suck-egg dog, but Jerry had hunted with her previously and said that he expected the blue tick would soon be the leader of his coonhound pack. He also said that he wasn't worried, since he enclosed his hens with high woven wire fences. Just a few weeks later, Jerry told my father that he had traded the Blue Tick to a foxhunter way over in the next county. He said the Blue Tick would run off whenever she was let out of his dog kennel, and even when they were out hunting, she would immediately run to some neighbor's henhouse looking for eggs. He was satisfied with the trade, however, indicating that he had doubled his initial investment in the Blue Tick, and her new owner was satisfied as well.

It seems a bit unfortunate, somehow, to have the customs, culture, and practices of having a collection of household chickens and hunting dogs, developed over several hundred years and enjoyed by so many people, totally disappear in an individual's lifetime. The demise of this culture began with the post-war advent of the production of cheap, synthetic nitrogen-based fertilizers, as the war industries converted from the production of munitions.

Government-subsidized agribusiness, the huge agricultural corporations powered by these cheap fertilizers, quickly overwhelmed the individual household farms which raised chickens and produced eggs. By the end of the Vietnam War, the practices of raising household chickens for food and commercial purposes by the rural population had basically ceased. So we are left with only a hollow remnant, with an echo from the Elvis Presley musical hit "You Ain't Nothing But a Hound Dog" to reflect the behavior of the rejected suck egg dog. The term "suck-egg dog" has long faded from our repertoire of insults, although I can recall using it at least once in my adult life, and the individual at whom the epithet was hurled actually seemed more puzzled than insulted.

Years later, my brother Jimmy was tragically devastated by mental illness. But even in his deepest misery, he would respond with a smile when we talked of our nights of possum hunting, or when I would remind him about his prediction of snow and my rash bet with the elaborate side conditions. He would sometimes reply to my attempt to engage him in conservation by reminiscing about the time when he tried to dislodge the hissing devil possum from the hickory tree by using his belt and shoe. But he would just shake his head sadly whenever I would talk of our little Blue Tick suck-egg dog.

The Parkway Bridge Over Mayberry Creek

The Parkway Through the Farm

"Grandma! Why is Grandpa crawling into that little cave under the Parkway?"

It was amazing to see my elderly grandfather crawling on his hands and knees and disappearing into a small, dark tunnel in the embankment beneath the Blue Ridge Parkway. As I watched him, he had first removed the heavy wooden door that covered the hole in the bank, then he got down on all fours in middle of the mucky little stream that trickled from the tunnel opening. Finally he crawled through the mud and weeds and vanished into the orifice under the highway. This could not have been an easy task for anyone, and it appeared to be especially hard for someone aged seventy-six. But after a disappearance of only a few minutes he emerged, backing out of the muddy wet hole in the earth, his hat covered with cobwebs and the legs of his overalls covered with black, sticky mud.

What is Grandpa doing in that cave? I asked my grandmother. I was a child of just seven, staying a few days with my grandparents, and Grandpa's behavior seemed really odd to me. Grandma attempted an explanation.

"The spring clogged up again. Your grandpa is cleaning it out."

"Spring? That hole under the parkway is a spring?" I thought springs bubbled up out of the ground, and most of them I had seen were inside little houses. How could there be a spring in a cave back under a highway?

Grandma stepped into the back of the house through the kitchen door and just as quickly stepped back out, shouting to my grandfather, who had just made his reappearance from the interior of the earth. He grunted mightily as he tried to get up on his feet, but Grandma was giving him a bad report.

" That didn't do the job, Dump. Try again."

Grandpa never complained much about anything. In this case, he just grumbled a bit under his breath, grunted back down onto his knees and again disappeared back into the black hole under the Parkway. In just a moment, Grandma stepped in and out of the kitchen and shouted from the back door again.

"That did it, Dump. It's running full again." (My grandfather, John Henry Yeatts was known as "Dump" to most folks in Mayberry, but I could tell he didn't like it much when anyone other than my grandmother used the nickname.)

Grandpa backed out of the damp hole again, attained a vertical stance and exhaled loudly as he slung mud from his hands and pulled on his wet, muddy overall legs. "Humph! Whada mess!" That was his only comment as he disappeared into the wash house to get the mud off his hands and put on dry overalls.

Grandma and Grandpa's house was built at the foot of a hill, and it is likely that the original builder chose the site because of the bold spring that emerged from the hillside. In the days before indoor plumbing, having one's house near a reliable source of water was perhaps the first consideration in selecting the building site for a rural home. Even if an older home had indoor plumbing added later, the spring often continued to be the source of water, with the pump often located in the spring house. But not in this case.

In 1898, when Grandpa and Great Uncle George purchased "the Moore Place" in Mayberry, the original three room house was already about twenty years old, and there was, among the several out buildings, a well-built little house covering the spring. Improvements in the spring house became an on-going project for Grandpa, almost from the time they first moved into the house. In the original the spring house, the water bubbled up from the ground into a stone cistern, a sunken box-shaped structure which served as a reservoir so that water could be easily dipped out by the bucket full. Grandpa added two long and shallow concrete troughs inside the spring house. The troughs maintained water at two different depths to provide cooling and storage for milk and perishable foods.

With the bold spring located a short distance up the hill, at an elevation of several feet above the house, it did not take my grandfather long to figure out that water could be piped from the spring directly into the house under the influence of gravity. A concrete cistern was constructed in a corner of the kitchen, basically a waist-high block of concrete formed around a cylindrical basin of about a ten gallon capacity. Water from the spring flowed into and out of the cistern continuously, day and night, winter and summer, so it never froze.

The water flowed into the cistern from the bottom and the overflow exited via a pipe near the top and out through the kitchen wall. A few years later, Grandpa built a spring house onto the end of the kitchen. The overflow from the cistern was piped through the wall into the spring house, and a door was cut through the kitchen wall to provide direct access from the kitchen into the spring house. Eventually, a side porch was closed in so that a bathroom could be added to the house. This gravity powered water system was something of a contraption, but it worked most of the time, once it was realized that the pipe to the house did not quite run continuously downhill all the way from the spring to the house, and that the water had be allowed to run all of the time for the siphoning of water from the spring to the house to be reliable. Electricity had not yet come to Mayberry, so by the standards of early twentieth century Appalachia, the Yeatts home, with its running water and indoor plumbing, represented a triumph in convenience and luxury, relatively speaking.

Rumors about the possible construction of some sort of new road that would run along the crest of the Blue Ridge Mountains from up near Washington, D.C. all the way to some unspecified point in South Carolina or Georgia had begun almost as soon as Roosevelt took office in 1933. One rumor was that the "gumment," as the State and Federal Governments were collectively and derisively referred to, was going to build a "farm to market" highway to benefit the farm economy of the Appalachian Region. Some of the more thoughtful Blue Ridge Mountain residents doubted the accuracy of that rumor. What did the Blue Ridge Mountains have to market? The chestnut trees were all dead, the market for apples was saturated, the sawmills could hardly give lumber away in the depression, and it was not likely that the government was going to intentionally assist in the distribution of illegal corn whisky.

Sometimes the route of the new road was rumored to be through Virginia and North Carolina, and sometimes the rumor was spread that the route had been changed to Kentucky and Tennessee and it would bypass Southwestern Virginia entirely. But those rumors which described a new highway which would function simply as a scenic drive for tourists through the Blue Ridge Mountains were dismissed as an idea too ridiculous for even the Government to consider. It was even suggested that the road might be a scenic highway from which commercial vehicles such as farm trucks and tractors would be excluded. The good folk of Mayberry held a pretty low opinion of the Government, but they could not imagine the Roosevelt Administration embarking on such a project with the country sunk so deep into economic depression. The new government project did not yet even have a name. It would be several years after the road was built before it was officially named the "Blue Ridge Parkway."

But when State Government Officials began contacting the land owners and then surveyors began appearing on the farms around Mayberry in the summer of 1935, it was clear that something out of the ordinary was about to happen. The state governments were given the task of acquiring the land, but county employees were the first to officially contact the affected residents in the Blue Ridge Region about the purchase of easements for a highway across their land. Federal Bureaucrats had correctly concluded that local and state officials would be more successful in negotiating with residents about obtaining rights-of-way across their land than officials from the Federal Government, although to many of the people affected, neither the State nor the Federal governments were entities which could be trusted.

The amount of money offered to the land owners for allowing the highway to be built across their farms and forests seems like a pittance today – three or and four hundred dollars was typical – but remember, this was in the midst of the Great Depression, when four hundred dollars would buy a new Model-A Ford. Grandpa Yeatts said that when the first officials from the Commonwealth of Virginia approached him an about easement across his farm in 1935, they wanted free reign to build the road across his property, with the precise route not yet even determined. They wanted him to sign an agreement that would give the government the right to build the road wherever future surveys indicated would be best, and specified a two hundred foot-wide right of way. All of this was in return for the grand sum of four hundred dollars. Grandpa may have spoken with a colloquial mountain dialect, but he was not stupid. He told them that there were a lot of details that would have to be worked out before he would give their offer any consideration.

My grandfather's position was this: there could be no negotiations until the precise route the road would take across his property was determined and mapped out for him to examine, and then they could begin discussing such details such as moving or replacing farm buildings and providing a connection between the two sides of his farm, which would be split asunder by the new highway. His objective was not to get as much money as possible, but to minimize the damage inflicted on the home and farm he had worked so hard to build. Rumors circulating by this time included stories of how the government was taking mountain peoples' homes with no negotiations and pitiful compensation. Some of these stories have been documented.

Fortunately, as the route of the scenic highway was mapped out, then modified again and again, the architects of the highway began to realize that these farms and homes and the mountain people themselves were an important part of the mountain scenery. The highway could display a historical view of a vanishing American Culture. As the project progressed, more effort was expended in creating a scenic highway which would cause a minimal disruption of rural Appalachian life and incorporate old-timey mountain farm scenery as a part of it. Once the land for the road had been obtained, the responsibility for supervising its construction was passed to The U.S. Department of the Interior. Local contractors and workers were employed to the greatest extent possible, making the construction of the Parkway a significant economic boon to the local economies.

Even though the route of the new highway was modified and the right of way narrowed, life was forever changed for my grandparents when the scenic highway was built through Mayberry. Although the right of way for the highway was reduced from two hundred feet to a hundred and fifty, the proposed center of the highway still was located only seventy-five feet from the back door of the house, and the embankment approached the house itself. When the Mayberry section of the Parkway was first opened, a Department of Interior right-of way sign was still nailed onto one of the posts supporting the roof of Grandma's back porch.

If the initial proposal had stood, the only way the Parkway route through Dump Yeatts's farm could have been any worse would have been for it to have taken the home. As it was, the right-of-way cut the farm in half, ran right through the apple orchard, took the main barn and the granary. Worst of all, the route went right over the spring house. When Grandpa obtained the assistance of Frank Burton, a lawyer from Stuart who had close ties to Senator Harry Bird, one of the early proponents of the Parkway, The Department of the Interior suddenly became a bit more flexible. They agreed to move the barn and granary to any reasonable location my grandfather selected, and an underpass connecting the parts of the farm on either side of the new road was to be included as a part of the design of the stone bridge over Mayberry Creek. The route was slightly modified so that the center of the road was a hundred feet and the property boundary moved to twenty-five feet from the house. The compensation for the property taken was raised to six-hundred dollars. But the spring remained a sticky issue.

The spring house was demolished and in its place, a concrete box was built around the spring. When the road fill was graded in, covering the concrete spring box, access to the spring was created via a horizontal square culvert, basically a tunnel. Never again was the spring to be an entirely satisfactory source of water for the home; the gravity water system could never be made to function as reliably as it had before the construction of the road. My elderly grandfather, almost to the end of his days, had to periodically crawl through the cold spring water into the tunnel under the Parkway to work his magic with the spring.

The government actually offered to dig a well and install a pump to replace the spring. But there was no electricity in Mayberry then, so the pump would have to be a hand pump, and that would mean the end of the running water system in the house. The concrete box surrounding the spring with access via the tunnel under the roadbed was a less than satisfactory solution to be sure, but it allowed Grandma and Grandpa to keep their running water.

The Department of the Interior kept most of its promises. Access between the separated halves of the farm was provided by a lane built beside Mayberry Creek. The lane and the creek together pass under the Parkway through the arch of a graceful stone bridge. Several of the farm structures were successfully moved, but the Parkway took several acres of good pastureland and most of the orchard.

Access to some of the fields was made quite inconvenient, and the farm just never seemed to function well after the construction of the Blue Ridge Parkway.

Grandpa often felt harassed by the Parkway Rangers; they seemed to be always telling him that either his bee hives or Grandma's garden or a grazing cow was intruding on Parkway land. Once, when a Ranger informed Grandpa that his bee hives were over on Parkway right of way, Grandpa told him, "If you don't like the location of the bee hives, then you just move them to wherever it suits you." The ranger decided to let the hives stay put. But by the time the Parkway through the farm was completed, Grandpa was almost seventy and he decided it was time to cut back on the farming anyway. He did, however, keep a couple of milk cows and Grandma kept her little flock of chickens for twenty more years.

The old home in Mayberry, now well over a hundred years old, continues to be used by some of the Yeatts grandchildren. Electricity came to Mayberry in 1949, and the spring in the tunnel under the Parkway, now assisted by an electric pump, continues to provide the water for the old Yeatts home.

The Mayberry Trading Post

A Mayberry Mystery

The customers looked as though they might bolt for the door when Gene came roaring up Mayberry Church Road in his old Dodge truck and pulled up to the side of the Mayberry Store. The military surplus truck, equipped with four wheel drive and no muffler, generated a din that could be mistaken for the roar of a WW II bomber. For the people inside the store, the noise created the sensation that the building itself was on the verge of taking flight.

The engine gave a loud backfire and the tail pipe belched a billow of gray smoke as the vehicle slid to a halt, stopping at an odd angle and occupying almost half of the small lot beside the store. But no matter that, for most week days from November to May, there was no need to be concerned about finding a place to park at the Mayberry Store. It was starting to rain, and there would be few tourists stopping in here on such a drizzly March afternoon.

The stocky driver of the truck, clad in his winter uniform of Carhart insulated overalls and an Atlanta Braves baseball cap, slid from the high cab of the truck. With a well-practiced maneuver, he slammed the truck door behind his back with a flick of a huge calloused hand, gave an arthritic grunt, and headed toward the front of the old store. He walked with his arms askew, rocking from side to side in a slightly stooped shuffle, typical of farm folk who have spent their lives engaged in hard work. Gene stopped by here about this time most days for crackers and a bottle of pop. Often he would hold council with Coy Lee, his life-long friend, second cousin once removed, and proprietor of the store. Today's visit, however, appeared to have a more definite purpose.

In recent years, a decline in the farming population in the area had coincided with an increase in tourist traffic on the nearby Blue Ridge Parkway. One effect of the change in the customer base was that mountain crafts and collectibles were now the store's most profitable stock. The change in merchandise and customers had also prompted a change in the wording on the high false front of the wooden store building. For the first half century of the store's existence, large, bold letters identified the structure as *Mayberry General Store*, and just below, in much smaller letters, *U.S. Post Office, Mayberry, Va.* In the 1930's the post office closed, the ownership changed, and the sign was changed to *Yeatts Brothers' Store.* Recently, the name had been changed again, this time to a more touristy, *Mayberry Trading Post.* Locally, it was rarely referred to as anything other than "The Mayberry Store."

The tattered "NO GAS" signs draped on the gas pumps did not bother to explain why the store has stopped selling gas. In the eighties, when Coy Lee began having trouble with the old metal underground fuel tanks, he decided that continuing in the fuel trade was not worth the effort. He had never much liked the idea of self-service gas, and when one is five-foot-six and weighs over three hundred pounds, continually getting up and going out front to dispense gas can be a burdensome chore.

But one thing had not changed. The service most appreciated by local patrons of The Mayberry Trading Post was its function as the clearing house for local news and gossip. But it was also the place where one could purchase staple grocery and hardware items and buy or sell locally produced jams and jellies, old-time music tapes, and assorted collectibles.

In recent years, books related to the Appalachian Culture had become one of the more popular items in the store. If someone expressed an interest in the local culture, especially with regard to the name "Mayberry," they might also receive an unsolicited lecture on local history and genealogy. A customer might also leave assured that they had just visited the real, original Mayberry, founded long before the Civil War by people whose surname was *Mayberry*. One also might receive a free brochure about the sights and scenes to be found in Mount Airy, North Carolina, only twenty miles away and the childhood home of Andy Griffin, creator of the fictional Mayberry.

Due to his slow talk and rural speech pattern, Coy Lee's observations were sometimes dismissed by people who did not know him, but he read voraciously and retained tomes of knowledge about local genealogy and history. Although he was a religious man, like many of us, he may have had an inclination to exaggerate the exploits of ancestors in the Revolutionary and Civil Wars.

Gene approached the front of the old store purposefully at first, but he then stopped short in front of the sagging double front door. For a moment he stood in front of the door with his head down, so deeply engrossed in thought that he appeared to be oblivious to the chilly March mist. Finally, he grasped the ancient iron door handle, pressed down on the thumb latch, and swung the door inward. The transition in passing from daylight into the interior of the narrow, dimly lit store was an experience similar to passing through the entrance to a mine. Gene paused again in the doorway to accustom his eyes to the dim interior while seeking out the area behind the middle of the left counter where he expected that Coy Lee would be seated.

"Why don'cha close that pneumonia hole?" came a grumble from behind the counter. Broad counters, topped with antique display cases and disorganized piles of tools, work clothes, books, cassette tapes, and an incredible array of new and used merchandise ran along of either side of the store. Across the narrow aisles behind the counters, eclectically stocked shelves sagged along the walls from floor to ceiling. Midway along the left-side counter, the one spot of uncluttered surface in the store defined Coy Lee's command center. The area was flanked by an old manual cash register to the right and by a goose-necked reading lamp to the left. Behind the cleared counter area, little more than a foot above the worn wooden counter surface, shone the round, bald head of the proprietor himself. At the moment, Coy Lee had his forearms braced on the counter top as he leaned close over his whittling. The object he was carving appeared to be a mountain lion.

"Howdy Gene," rumbled Coy Lee without looking up from his work. "Don't look much like spring's quite got here yet."

"Feels like it's headed back 'tother way." responded Gene. Their daily ritual of weather-related greetings varied only in response to current conditions. For a while, Gene stood back, waiting for the two customers in the store, people he did not know, to leave. As soon as the strangers were gone, Gene located a tall wooden stool further down the counter and dragged it to a spot directly in front of Coy Lee. He disappeared for just a moment, returning with a pack of cheese crackers and an opened bottle of Pepsi. Coy Lee stopped whittling long enough to make an entry in a spiral bound account book while Gene sat silent, except for the rustle of the wrapper and the crunching of the crackers. Even after the crackers were gone and the wrapper tossed, Gene continued to sit silently, appearing to be fascinated by Coy Lee's whittling. For a time, the only sounds in the store were the hum of the drink cooler and the scrape of Coy Lee's pocket knife. When he finally looked up across the counter at Gene, Coy Lee could see that Gene was in an unusually serious mood.

"You doin' OK?" Coy Lee wondered aloud. He already knew what the response would be, but the silence needed to be broken.

"Ahhh, this danged weather's killin' me." Gene gave his standard bad-weather response, and the silence resumed for a long minute. Then Gene unbuttoned the breast pocket of his flannel shirt, stuffed his large hand down into it and fumbled around, finally withdrawing a tiny object. His thumb and forefinger concealed the object almost entirely until, without a word, he plunked it down on the counter top, right beside Coy Lee's object d'art. Coy Lee leaned over the dime-sized object and squinted, then picked it up and held it close in front of his eyes. Adjusting the position of his glasses, he first held the tiny object up under the lamp, then moved it in front of his mouth and exhaled onto it heavily. "Hah! Haaah!" After polishing the object briskly on his shirt sleeve he returned it to the counter.

Coy Lee continued to study the object for a time, squinting his eyes and pursing his mouth. Every moment or two he would reach over with his forefinger and rotate the object about a quarter-turn, first one way and then the other, then he would flip the object over, causing it to flash brightly under the lamp

Finally, Coy Lee raised his head, rolled his eyes up at Gene, and cryptically rendered his verdict. "Five dollar gold piece, half-eagle. Philadelphia, 1873. They're probably worth 'bout a hunnert dollars these days.

Gene did not comment on Coy Lee's appraisal, but began another search of his overall pockets. "Well then, whad'a ya think of this?" Gene twisted his hand down into the large pocket in the bib of his overalls and retrieved a dull, dirty oval shaped object. The three-inch-long object fitted neatly into his palm as he passed it under Coy Lee's tracking eyes and allowed it to slide from his hand, onto the counter top beside the gold piece.

Coy Lee recoiled from the counter with surprise. "Why, that looks like a Union Army belt buckle!" Leaning back over the counter, he moved the oval object toward the lamp, while his other hand brushed off dirt which had fallen from the object onto the counter. The letters "US" on the object were clearly visible, and although it was colored a dull green from corrosion, it was rust-free and most likely made of brass. It appeared to Coy Lee to be genuine, but as he searched for a foundry mark that might confirm its origin, Gene was struggling to retrieve something from the deep, narrow pocket on the right leg of his overalls.

"And then, how's about this?" Gene pulled an amorphous lump from his overall tool pocket and deposited it on the counter, where it shed a layer of dirt and rust. The lump was vaguely shaped like a revolver, but what should have been the cylinder was fused into the frame in a mass of mossy rust, and what might have been a barrel was just a rusty extension truncated a few inches in front of the frame. There were no hand grips visible, and only an intact brass trigger guard provided clear evidence that the object had once been a firearm.

"Well now, that there ain't worth nothin'," Coy Lee grumped, pushing the lump aside and starting to flick some of the debris off the counter top with the side of his hand. Returning to his examination of the belt buckle, Coy Lee moved the buckle back and forth under the lamp, while Gene sat on the stool in front of the counter, silently rocking back and forth.

"Are you wanting to sell this stuff?" It appeared to Coy Lee that Gene had not brought this booty into the "Trading Post" to see if he would buy it.

"Well, I'd sell it if the price was right. But mainly, I just wanted to see what you think about it. What kind of old gun is that? And is that buckle for real?"

"All I can tell you about this here..." Coy Lee condescended to take another look at the lump, is that it used to be some kind of pistol. Probably it was an Iver Johnson Owl Head, but it's just junk now. Now, if this buckle is genuine, it's worth pretty good money, but they's lots of fakes around. Where'd you get this stuff?"

"I found it, and you'll never guess where." responded Gene, leaning forward and staring at Coy Lee, trying to appear both ominous and wise.

Coy Lee responded with a dismissive shrug. "All in the same place?"

"All within about a foot of one another," Gene said.

Then Gene stood up and leaned in over the counter until he was speaking to the top of Coy Lee's head. "Under Granpa's barn, that's where I found 'em. Under my granddaddy's barn." He spoke in a low voice, glancing furtively around, as though there might be other listeners hidden somewhere in the store. "Under yore Uncle Jace's old barn!"

"Jace's old barn?" Coy Lee's mouth dropped open. "Up on the Dickerson place?"

"They was all under that barn." affirmed Gene, nodding as he sat back proudly. "Under Granpa's cow barn."

Coy Lee really didn't have a response, but after a minute the silence had to be broken. His voice was hoarse, as though he had a lump in his throat. "Well, I think maybe we can figger out how they got there. But then, how come you to find 'em?"

Gene began to explain to Coy Lee about how he had pushed the dilapidated old barn down a few weeks ago, and just this morning, he had begun leveling the spot where the old barn had been with his front-end loader. There, he planned on putting up a new silo and feed mixer for the dairy farm. "The pistol was the first thing I seen. I got off the tractor to see what it was, and when I decided it was a pistol, I started scraping around with a shovel, looking for more stuff. What I found next was a couple of horseshoes and 'bout a dozen nails. But then I got down and started goin' through the dirt I dug up by hand. That's when I pulled out the gold piece and then the buckle. By hand."

"How deep did you dig?" Coy Lee wanted to know.

"Not too deep. After I found the coin, I scraped around all over the place, hopin' to find more. Then I found the belt buckle and I got to thinking, thinking maybe I'd dig up some bones, but I didn't. I don't really want to go digging up bones. I may not dig no deeper. I may just tamp 'er down and pour the slab on top of what I've got dug now, just like she is, and not go diggin' any deeper."

"Well then, I guess you must have heard about what some folks said happened when Uncle Jace was building that barn." Coy Lee made the statement sound like a question.

"I've heard it, several times. Two or three different tales." answered Gene. "Pappy told me the tale, and you told it to me. But I really didn't think much of it 'til now."

In rural communities such as Mayberry, farms often continue for generations to be known by the name of some long-departed, previous owner. The part of Gene's farm where the old barn had stood was still known to the locals as "The Dickerson Place," although Gene had owned it for several decades and Coy Lee's family had owned it for years before that.

At the time that Gene bought the property, he and Coy Lee had talked a little about the family rumor. Gene had not mentioned it to a soul since, but there were some other folks around who knew the story and would occasionally bring it up to Coy Lee, who would discuss it willingly. In spite of having just been told by Gene that he knew the story, Coy Lee felt compelled to repeat the entire saga, just to make sure that Gene had all the details. Coy Lee was an accomplished teller of tales and a pretty good amateur historian, although he might sometimes mix historical fact with local folklore. He usually liked to begin his stories by laying out what he considered to be the proper historical foundation.

Coy Lee started. "You know that Uncle Jace was born in 1840?"

Gene nodded in agreement.

"And that he fought in the civil war?" Again Gene nodded and added a little history of his own.

"Him and five of his brothers. Uncle Charles was killed in that war."

"You know that he was taken as a prisoner of war and kept in the camp at Elmira for almost a year? And that he nearly died there? And that it took him a month to walk back home after the war." To each new detail Gene nodded an affirmation.

"Ev Wood helped him build that barn. Ev was born about 1872, just a kid when they built it." Coy Lee droned on and on, giving details about each of the protagonists, until at last he began to get into the real story. "I think they raised that barn about 1890."

"Eighteen eighty-eight was what was carved into the door post." Gene was pleased to be able to correct Coy Lee on a detail. "They said that Ev Wood was good at riving shingles, so Grandpa hired him to help put on the roof." As Coy Lee moved further into the tale, more and more of the details became attributed to the ubiquitous "they."

"They said that Uncle Jace was up on the roof toward the back side of the barn and Ev was sittin' in front riving shingles when Ev seen this man a-walkin' up the hill from a long ways off. He yelled to Uncle Jace that there was somebody coming up the road, but right then, neither one of 'em thought much about it."

Gene began to lean forward on the stool in anticipation. It was a story that he already knew, but Coy Lee was good at telling his tales and so far, he was relating the story pretty much as Gene knew it. Coy Lee continued. "Uncle Jace was up on the back side of the roof, nailin' down shingles when this stranger walks up to Ev and yells out, real loud, 'Is there a Mister Jace Barnard to be found

around these parts?' Of course, Uncle Jace looked over the
ridge of the barn roof to see who it was."

"When the stranger saw Uncle Jace, he ran around
the barn to where the ladder was set up and yelled up at
him, 'Well, I finally found you, you snake-in-the-grass!
Now I aim to collect what I'm owed.'"

Uncle Jace yells back to the stranger, "I don't owe
you nothin'. Now you'd just best be gettin' on up the road."

The stranger and Uncle Jace yelled and cussed at
one another for several minutes, Uncle Jace on the roof and
the stranger on the ground. Finally the stranger yelled, "I
aim to collect what I'm owed," and started climbing up the
ladder. As he got to the top and started to step off the
ladder onto the roof, he jerked out a pistol. That was really
dumb, 'cause Uncle Jace was standin' right there at the top
of the ladder holdin' his roofing hammer, and when he seen
the gun, he just swung the hammer around and whacked the
stranger up side the head. The stranger fell backwards and
hit the ground, head first. They said that he never moved
after he fell, never even twitched!"

At this point, Gene decided it was time for him to
take over and introduce Coy Lee to his version of the tale.

"Ev and Grandpa had a hard time figgerin' out
what to do with the dead man. Ev always claimed that he
wanted to notify the sheriff, but back then it took most of a
day to ride to the county seat. It may not have even been
clear if the barn was in Patrick or Floyd county. Either way,
it'd take another day for the sheriff to ride back here, and
the corpse would be rotting by then. Unless they put the
body in the spring house, and what if Grandma or the kids
found a dead man in the spring house?

It was a clear case of self-defense, but even if the
sheriff agreed, there still might have been a hearing at the

court house and all, and that would have taken two or three days. Grandpa and Ev finally just decided to bury him under the new barn. The ground was already dug up anyway, and there would be nothing to show that somebody was buried there."

Coy Lee decided it was his turn again.

"Ev said that he was real worried about the whole thing, but he wasn't gonna' do a whole lot of arguing with Jace Barnard when he was all riled up. It would have made sense for them to bury the pistol with the body. It's not likely that they searched the body, even to try and find out who he was. Jace and Ev, they wouldn't have kept anything the man had. That wouldn't of been right. They said the man was dressed real poorly. His shoes were plumb wore out and his pistol had just three cartridges in it."

At this point, Coy Lee began scraping on the front of what appeared to be the cylinder of the rusty lump. When a piece of rusty metal broke away, revealing the tip of a lead bullet they agreed that continuing to scrape might cause the entire mass to disintegrate, and determining the number of bullets actually in the gun was not all that important, so he just continued with his rambling story.

"Ev said he asked Uncle Jace if he knew the man, and he said Uncle Jace told him, "Oh Yes! I know the rascal well!" But that was all that he would ever say.

When Uncle Jace got back home, they said Aunt Adeline told him, "Some strange feller was by here earlier. Said he had some business he wanted to talk about with you. Did he ever find you?"

"Yes, he did." Uncle Jace is said to have told her. "We got our business all done." "

Coy Lee seemed to have finished the story, but Gene still had a lot of questions.

"But who was he?" Gene protested. "Grandpa must have told Ev who the man was, or at least why he was looking for him!"

"Don't think so." Coy Lee shook his head. "I don't think he ever told anybody, I don't think he ever said another word about it.   Some said that the man was a soldier that Uncle Jace had known in the war and they had a falling out over a card game. Others claimed that he was a Yankee solder that he had wounded. Who knows?   The man claimed that Uncle Jace owed him something, probably money. Maybe he thought Uncle Jace had cheated him."

"Well, the feller must not have been from around here." Gene observed. "Nobody ever came looking for him. I did hear rumors about a Yankee who came snooping around here one time after the war and was never heard from again."

"Oh, folks were always tellin' tales like that. But it's true that this man's shoes was all wore out," emphasized Coy Lee, "like he'd come from a long ways off."

As he got wound up again, Coy Lee's revelations became ever more bizarre. "Uncle Jace used to tell that he was a sniper in the war, and it's likely that he was. He used to tell that before they were overrun at Gettysburg, he was a sniper positioned up in a tree. I heard one story where he spotted a Union soldier in the woods peeing, and he shot the man's pekker off. He was a good enough shot to have done that. Maybe it was that man."

Gene couldn't buy that theory. "That don't make no sense, Coy Lee. Most likely, a man would bleed to death from a wound like that. And how would a soldier ever find out who was the sniper from the other side who shot him at some particular time and place in the war? And he wanted money. How much would you rekon he thought his pekker was worth?"

Coy Lee did a quick calculation in his head. "Twenty-five years is pretty late to come-a-lookin' for somebody, even for somebody who done something to you like that."

"Unless it was twenty-five years before he could walk right," added Gene, as an afterthought. They both snickered at this bit of cruel humor.

"Well, nobody really knows, now do they. Now this here....," Coy Lee said as he held up the belt buckle, "would make it seem like maybe they were on opposite sides in the war, but it may have just been something he found when he needed to hold his pants up. There was more than two million of them made. And I never heard that anyone said the man talked like a Yankee."

Coy Lee put the buckle back down. "But you're right. It ain't likely somebody from the war would come looking for a man twenty-five years later, no matter how bad the blood. Personally, I just think the poor man was crazy."

"Well, should we tell somebody?" Gene wondered. "Should we notify the sheriff or the historical society or somebody?"

"Well now, that's up to you," allowed Coy Lee, "but if it was me, I'd put this stuff away where it'd never again see the light of day. If word gets out that there's stuff like this on your place, there'll be people sneaking around your barn lot with picks and shovels and metal detectors. If the Daughters of The Confederacy or the Historical Society finds out, they might declare it a historical site." He was only half serious.

"There's no statute of limitations on manslaughter, you know, not even a hundred years," Coy Lee continued, "but so far, you ain't found no human remains. It could be that your grandpa really did owe the man money and his heirs could still try to collect. There could be all kinds of complications. What if the government was to decide to dig for remains? You might never get your silo built."

Gene was in a terrible conundrum as the two sat in silence, meditating over the morbid relics. Then he had a thought. "How much would you give me for all this stuff?"

Coy Lee surveyed the objects again. "Well, I'd just throw that old piece of a pistol away. But, mmmm, I'll give you a hundred dollars for the gold piece and maybe... oh, another fifty for the belt buckle."

"I think them Union Army brass belt buckles go for about two-hundred, maybe two-fifty." Gene countered, slightly offended.

"I ain't completely sure that it's the real thing. But assuming it is a real Union Army Civil War buckle, I'll give you two hundred for everything." Coy Lee had made his final offer.

Gene slumped on the stool and stroked the stubble on his chin for couple of minutes. Suddenly he reached over and picked up the coin and the belt buckle from the counter top and placed them in the breast pocket of his overalls. Then he returned the piece of a firearm to the tool pocket.

"I think maybe I'll just hang on to this stuff for a while. It'll only get more valuable with time," Gene pronounced, as he carefully buttoned his pocket, then turned and walked to the front of the store.

As the old 4x4 roared and rattled out of the Trading Post parking lot, Gene made the observation that it was raining harder now, with maybe a little snow mixed in. The weather was just too rotten for him to get back to work on his new project today, and besides, he might just decide to dig around over that old barn site a little more before he poured any concrete.

Mayberry Singing

The Mayberry Presbyterian Church sits beside the Blue Ridge Parkway in the mountains of southwestern Virginia near milepost 180, about three miles south of Meadows of Dan. Today the church is a fieldstone-covered photographic icon, but until about sixty years ago, it was a classical wooden structure covered with plain white clapboards on the outside and white beaded chestnut ceiling on the inside. For many years, the rows of uncomfortable, straight-backed, home-built benches told of the limited means of the congregation at the time of the church's construction.

Today the church is equipped with comfortable cushioned pews and carpet on the floor, but otherwise it remains small and simple. Except for the addition of the vestibule on to the front, it is the same basic structure where I sometimes attended services as a child, more than sixty years ago.

Electric power bypassed Mayberry until after World War II, so in my earliest memories, lighting in the church was provided by four Aladdin kerosene lamps mounted on wall sconces. There was a fifth Aladdin lamp, one with a shade, suspended over the pulpit by a chain, but I think it was seldom used. Musical accompaniment was provided by a well-used upright piano and/or a pump organ whenever there was someone present who could play either of them. In the winter, a pot-bellied cast iron stove with a stovepipe that ran up to the ceiling sat directly in front of the plain home-built wooden pulpit. On a cold morning, it could provide just enough heat to make sitting through the service tolerable. In the summer, the stove was removed from the building to provide a better view of the preacher.

The small louvered steeple, which sat on the roof right above the front door, contained a bell of modest size and amazing volume. Or perhaps it is more of a testimony to the quietness of that particular time and place that whenever the bell was rung, it would summon members of the community from every direction, some from nearly a mile.

The folks in Mayberry knew to listen for the bell on Sunday mornings, as it was first rung a half-hour in advance, just to let the people know that there was to be a service that day and to give everyone time to get ready. The minister was a circuit rider with several other churches, and with bad weather and unpaved roads, the precise time of the service was never very certain. If the bell was rung at some time other than a Sunday morning, it was because there was either a community emergency or some special event. On one such occasion, the people of The Mayberry were surprised and concerned to hear the church bell insistently ringing on a Thursday evening in June of 1945.

By the summer of 1945, the Germans had been beaten, but the war with Japan appeared deadlier than ever and there were no GI's coming home yet. Like most small communities, as the war continued to drag on, more and more of the young men we knew became casualties. On the home front, many basic necessities such as canning jars and sugar became quite scarce, but that seemed pretty minor compared with the suffering of people in much of the world.

That may be why, the minister, Bob Childress, and Frank Shelor, a musically talented resident of Meadows of

Dan, got together and decided that the community needed a spiritual uplift and that a Gospel Singing at the Mayberry Church would surely help. Many people in Mayberry and Meadows of Dan had no means of transportation, so the organizers split up a large area of "the top of the mountain" between them, with Bob Childress canvassing the areas to the west of Mayberry toward Laurel Fork and Bell Spur, and Frank Shelor taking responsibility for the area east of Mayberry, toward Meadows of Dan and Vesta. They both knew that some of the folks in the surrounding community would have little interest in a Gospel Singing, and that more had work which would prevent their attendance. But they were sure that many would come.

Although Frank Shelor was a staunch Missionary Baptist, his love of music took precedent over theology, especially when the community was in need. Frank was a talented individual who could play several musical instruments, had an excellent bass singing voice, and could sight read either shape notes or staff. And he had been organizing gospel singings in the area for years.

There was really no simple way for word of the singing to be spread in advance, as only a few people in Meadows of Dan and Mayberry had telephones. All the organizers could do was to spend the afternoon before the singing driving around telling people about the event; if they were interested, someone would be by to pick them up in a couple of hours. This was barely enough forewarning to allow anyone who was interested in attending to get the cows milked, the kids fed, and their faces washed. There was no way of knowing just how many would attend.

Our house was one of Frank Shelor's first stops on the night of the singing. Four from our house joined Mr. Shelor, his wife Betts, and their youngest son Otto, in their

1937 Chevrolet pickup for the pilgrimage to Mayberry. They were my mom (Dad was away fighting in the Pacific at the time), my ten year old sister and me, and a twelve year old cousin who was spending the summer with us. The cousin happened to have a fine singing voice, and the fact that he was a Jewish kid from New Jersey seemed to not dampen his enthusiasm for singing along with Southern Christian Gospel Music in the least.

From Meadows of Dan, Frank drove down the Mayberry Road toward the church, stopping next at Grover Reynolds's home. Grover was too busy to join us, but his wife Stella, daughter Louise, and son Galen, all joined us in the pickup. Stella was noted for her strong alto voice, Galen could sing either tenor or lead, and Louise, though barely a teenager, was a pretty good gospel pianist. Mr. Shelor could hardly contain his enthusiasm; with Louise and my mom both attending, there would be someone to play both the piano and the organ.

Just down the Mayberry Road from the Reynolds's, the pickup turned right and crossed over the parkway, driving down Maple Swamp Road to pick up Mrs. Maggie Wood and her daughter, Margaret. Margaret's older brothers, Benton and Marlin were at home, but they had too much work that had to be done to go to the singing.

Instead, while Maggie and Margaret got ready, the boys led all of the kids down to the spring house where they showed off the very large catfish their dad had caught several weeks before and they were now keeping in the spring box. Benton impressed all us younger kids by pointing out the "stinger" on catfish's back and giving us dire warnings about how carefully a catfish had to be handled when caught and what could happen if one happened to step on a catfish in the creek. Although I had never seen a catfish in the creeks around there, the warning was sufficiently frightening to put an end to my wading for the rest of the summer.

Maggie, lugging her autoharp, and Margaret piled on board. There were now three passengers in the cab and nine in the back, but Frank did not consider that a full load. He stopped next at a house at the other end of Maple Swamp, and although we were now only half of a mile from the church, Doris Wood and Agnes Pendelton joined us there, riding the short distance to the church seated on the lowered tailgate of the pickup, their feet dangling almost to the level of the dusty road.

Other than Mr. Shelor, who was beyond the age for military service, there were no adult men in our group. There was a war going on, and all the men who were not away in military service or employed in defense jobs in Radford or Roanoke had been hard at work on the farm all day and were just too tired to be uplifted.

The doors to the Mayberry Church were wide open when we got there, and the church was more than half full. A notice had been posted at the Mayberry Store and Mr. Childress had rung the bell earlier, so a large number of people were there who had come from walking distance. And as we waited, the lights of kerosene lanterns and flash lights carried by more folks converging on the church could be seen in both directions up and down the Mayberry Road. Some others I can recall being present were Mrs. Ella Scott and her grandson, Vernon Bolt and Mrs. Sally Spangler, with her grandson, Arnold Terry. Arnold, who was only twelve or thirteen, was already pretty good on the guitar and had brought his instrument along. After a welcome and a prayer from Reverend Childress, the entire congregation sang a few songs, traditional, upbeat hymns which everyone knew. I don't actually remember what we were singing at the beginning, but I somehow imagine that I can recall the group singing *Bringing in the Sheaves* and *Come Thou Fount,* maybe not really the rousing songs that one would normally associate with a gospel singing, but joyous and inspiring, songs well known to Baptist and Presbyterian alike.

At some point in the singing, sisters Margie and Bernice Spangler treated the congregation to a duet rendition of *Life's Railway to Heaven.* Frank Shelor, along with Otto on the mandolin and Arnold Terry on the guitar did a rousing presentation of *I'm Telling the World About His Love.* As soon as that song was ended, Otto burst into *Goin' Down This Road Feelin' Bad,* but Frank put a quick stop to that.

An impromptu quartet was assembled with Stella Reynolds as alto, Maggie Wood singing lead, Arnold Terry singing a pre-teen tenor, and Frank Shelor singing bass. Frank's voice was positively booming as they brought the singing to a close by singing *Let Us Have a Little Talk With Jesus* and *Turn Your Radio On.* By the time all of the impromptu groups had performed and the congregation sung a few closing songs, it must have then been almost ten o'clock, a really late hour for folks in Mayberry.

Everyone filed out into the church yard while Mr. Childress stood on the top step at the front of the Church, holding high a kerosene lantern to help everyone get started on their trip home. Those of us depending on Frank Shelor for our ride home had already piled into his truck, but when he finally climbed in under the steering wheel, turned on the ignition, and mashed his foot down on the starter pedal, absolutely nothing happened.

Mr. Shelor climbed out of the truck, folded up the louvered hood, and peered down into the darkness. He extracted a flashlight and a pair of pliers from the glove compartment and performed the precision battery check of shorting out the battery terminals with the plier handles. This procedure produced no spark at all, indicating a completely dead battery. Mr. Shelor then organized all of the younger members into a party which pushed the pickup down the sloping church driveway, while he steered the truck and popped the clutch. Almost immediately the engine caught and cranked. Success! But when Mr. Shelor turned the headlights on, the engine quickly shut down.

The process was repeated a couple more times as we pushed the pickup down the dark Mayberry road. Each time the engine started up when Frank would release the clutch, but then instantly shut off when the headlights were turned on. The diagnosis was that the battery was so far gone, the truck simply could not run and also power the headlights. Stuff like that happened all the time during the war years.

Some members of the party began to make alternate plans. Agnes, Doris, Maggie and Margaret decided it would be no problem for them to walk the half-mile over the hill to Maple Swamp. But those of us who lived in Meadows of Dan would have a four mile walk, a bit of a stretch on a dark night, and unfortunately, the few other motor vehicles at the church were already gone! What were we to do?

On this moonless night, Frank decided that with no lights, the best bet would be for him to drive back to Meadows of Dan on the Blue Ridge Parkway. The Parkway and the Mayberry Road ran approximately parallel from Mayberry to Meadows of Dan, but neither had a white center line. The Mayberry road was mostly one lane, and the Parkway was so new that the war had begun before the center line got painted. But the Parkway was, if you can believe it, considerably less curvy than the Mayberry Road, and it ran along a ridge much of the way. Maybe the starlight would help him see.

The batteries in Mr. Shelor's flashlight were also nearing the end of their life, but our cousin Joey was drafted into sitting on the right front fender of the truck and holding it. Trucks and cars from the 1930's had their headlights located in tear drop shaped nacelles mounted over the front fenders on either side of the hood. Joey sat on the fender, with his left leg squeezed under the headlight and his feet braced against the front bumper, holding tightly to the hood ornament with his left hand and clutching the flashlight with his right.

We eased along the black surface of the Parkway with everyone's eyes straining in the darkness. Mr. Shelor instructed Joey to leave the failing flashlight off until he called for light; then he was to turn the light on and direct it down toward the right shoulder of the road, so that maybe he would be able to distinguish the border between the pavement and the grass.

Once our eyes all became accustomed to the darkness, things went much better than we had feared. Even though there was no moon at all, the clear night sky was brilliant with stars. And never, before or since, have I seen such an incredible number of fireflies flashing their display. Mr. Shelor drove very slowly, of course, and he only had to call for the feeble assistance from the flashlight two or three times during the entire trip from Mayberry to Meadows of Dan.

I began the ride home with great concern, being especially fearful over the prospect of having to cross over the hundred-foot high Round Meadow bridge in the darkness. But the night was magical, the edges of the road were mostly visible, and we never seemed to be in any real danger. The starry skies and the firefly displays were so beautiful that I was actually sorry when we finally arrived in Meadows of Dan.

I am not really sure how much the light from the fireflies contributed to our safe trip home, but when we stopped in front of Stella Reynolds's house, she got out and walked around to the driver's window in the pickup, where she gave her brother Frank a testimony of total sincerity. "Frank," she told him, her voice quavering with emotion. "the singing was truly a blessing for all of us, and we have you to thank for that. But it surely was the Lord that sent all those lightning bugs tonight, just so you could deliver us all safely home."

And who could possibly disagree?

FUTILITY

John Hassell Yeatts

You gave me strength to heave the line,
    to pull the oar with force.
You placed me on a sturdy ship,
    but plotted not my course.
You gave me voice with which to sing,
    and that could not be wrong.
But in the haste of giving,
    you taught me not a song.

You launched my ship on stormy seas,
    pitting me against their might,
And without a crew or helmsman
    I sailed into the night.
It mattered not, the starless sky,
    I faced it without fear.
For thou did make me strong of heart
    and I was young in years.

I believed the coming dawn
    would bring a port to sight.
My voyage would be completed
    and ended so my plight.
But come the dawn, alas I found,
    to my complete dismay,
The fog had closed around me;
    there was no tranquil bay.

Opening Day

Mayberry was well-known as a trout fishing destination from as far back as I can remember, sportsmen driving into the area around Mayberry from miles away to fish in the Dan River and Round Meadow Creek. Those streams were known to have been well stocked with rainbow and brown trout by the *Virginia Department of Wildlife and Inland Fisheries*. Sometimes, the number of people out for fishing on opening day would be so large that the more accessible banks of the best fishing streams would be literally lined with fishermen.

One Year, the fishing crowd at Round Meadow Creek was so large that one Mayberry resident, Allen Spangler, gave up trying to fish and disgustedly walked up to the Mayberry Store to get something to eat. When asked how his fishing had gone, Allen, known for his unusual sense of humor, complained that he had spent all morning walking up and down the banks of Round Meadow Creek, just looking for a bow-legged man. When asked what he meant by that strange statement, he explained, "because that was the only way I could have ever got my dadgummed fishing pole out over the creek."

Stocked trout tend to migrate upstream from where they are released, many of them finding their way from the stocked streams into the smaller tributaries. This meant that less well-known streams such as Mayberry Creek, Tuggles Creek, and Maple Swamp Branch were being also stocked, but indirectly. Many of the local folks preferred to fish in these smaller streams, since they were not so heavily fished by people from outside the area. Those who really knew their Mayberry fishing could often catch trout that been swimming in the creek for a year or two. Trout that have lived in the wild for a while become more brightly colored and develop firmer flesh than recently released hatchery fish, and they are definitely better tasting. This distinction was probably more important to the locals, many of whom fished for food. The tourists primarily fished for sport and size was the primary consideration. For fishers who knew the area well, it was usually not difficult to catch enough trout for a good meal, whether the streams were stocked or not. And for some, it mattered little whether it was in or out of trout season.

Most of the stocked fish were either rainbow trout, initially an import from the Pacific West Coast, or the brown trout, originally brought in from Europe. Both of these varieties do quite well in the cold, swift waters of the Appalachian Mountain streams, and the brown trout especially, can grow to be quite large. This makes fishermen happy, but the only true native trout, the one prolific in the creeks and streams of the Blue Ridge Mountains a century ago, was the little brook trout.

A brook trout was a rare catch in the mountain streams of Virginia by the time I was old enough to fish, but my grandmother used to talk about how, as a child in the 1890's, her impoverished family really depended on the brook trout that she and her brothers would catch in Maple Swamp Branch and Round Meadow Creek. At the time, so many of the adults I knew had their dubious fishing tales, that I really did not take Grandma's stories about fishing as seriously as perhaps I should have.

My grandmother's brother, Len Reynolds had a great deal to do with Mayberry's fame as a trout fishing area. He worked there as a game warden and a fishing guide, and in that capacity he established strong friendships with many politicians in the region who also happened to be trout fishermen. When the State Government began stocking trout streams, the amount of fish stocked in a particular area was strongly influenced by political connections, and Len Reynolds had long-standing associations with some politicians from Stuart and Martinsville who could influence the distribution of the stocked trout. There was even a local saying to the effect that "the fish follow the politicians," and if certain politicians lost their elections, the fish went to another district.

In the middle of the last century, Christmas was the most significant holiday for the children who lived in the Blue Ridge Mountains, just as it was to the rest of the country. But the second most important holiday must surely have been the opening day of trout season. I call opening day a holiday because, back when trout season officially opened at daylight, school did not open until noon and even then, school attendance was pretty poor. A few years later, when trout season began officially opening at noon, school was dismissed at eleven a.m. on opening day, in response. In case you are wondering, Independence Day and the Southern States Cooperative Annual Stock Holder's Meeting were the holidays tied for third place. Thanksgiving was an important day too, but it was not exactly considered a holiday, since most of the folks I knew used Thanksgiving either for killing hogs or for cutting firewood, depending upon the weather.

I'll admit to not having been a skilled fisherman, either as a child or as an adult. As a child, I was not very patient when fishing, and my Dad was not very patient when he was trying to teach me. In fairness, Dad worked awfully hard, holding down a job which was full time and more, and then trying to farm on the side. He really didn't have a lot of time for frivolous stuff like teaching his kids to fish. Tuggles Creek ran right beside our house, though, and I was usually able to catch a fish or two on opening day, and I would occasionally catch fish for a couple of months after trout season opened, until the weather got warm. Never, however, did I even come close to catching the then legal limit of eight in one day, like so many of my school chums claimed to have done. Admittedly, as I was describing my fishing exploits to my friends, there were occasions when the number of fish I reported catching was exaggerated.

My most successful opening day trout fishing adventure actually occurred when I was about eight and my older sister was twelve. Our Mom was expecting a baby soon and was not feeling well at all, so my sister and I were staying in Mayberry with our grandparents, Dump and Edna Yeatts, for a few days. Although we were only three miles from home, I felt pretty homesick and unhappy, especially when it looked to me like I was not going to get to go fishing on opening day. Our sympathetic grandmother, upon learning what was wrong, suggested that she could take us fishing on the first morning of trout season.

I was not especially excited by Grandma's offer. I didn't have any fishing stuff with me, I wasn't sure that there were any fish in Mayberry Creek, and what on earth could my elderly and overweight grandmother possibly know about fishing anyway? But Grandma was insistent; the evening before the season opening, Grandpa helped us select and cut three straight and flexible hickory sprouts for fishing poles, each six or seven feet long. (I was twelve years old before I ever laid my hands on a store-bought rod and reel.) Grandma found some hooks and line that appeared to have been stored away for years, but I thought the hooks were too small for the size of any fish I intended to catch. Grandpa made us some lead sinkers by cutting the slugs off of twenty-two caliber bullets. He also optimistically cut us a hefty fish stringer from a forked birch twig. It looked like we really were going fishing!

My sister and I dug earth worms out from under cow pies and collected crickets from the woodshed, while Grandma, with a mysterious smile on her face, wandered into a grove of alders down near what we called "the creek bottom" at dusk. She was carrying a green glass canning jar and she announced that she was looking for her secret fishing bait.   All I had ever fished with was worms, crickets, and grubs, and I couldn't imagine what Grandma knew that I didn't.

Grandma was up by five o'clock every morning, and the day fishing season opened, she had us rousted out of bed, dressed, and shivering on the back porch before the first crack of daylight. We had not even eaten yet, since Grandma assured us that we were going to have fried trout for breakfast that morning.

We could hardly see where we were going, but Grandma led the way, using her fishing pole as a walking stick and carrying the mysterious canning jar and the birch fish stringer in the other hand. We tramped across the meadow and through the wet grass to the banks of Mayberry Creek, stopping above the wooden bridge where Mayberry Road crossed the creek and the stream tumbled over some large rocks into a small pool. It was just the beginning of daylight.

"Let's try here," Grandma suggested, and then

began whispering instructions about how to never let your shadow fall on the water and don't make too much noise and stuff like that. To this day, I do not know if fish even have ears, but everyone always seems to talk in whispers when they are trout fishing.

As I began baiting my hook with a worm and my sister was baiting hers with a cricket, Grandma retrieved an invisible something from the canning jar and used it to bait her hook. Almost before we had gotten our bait wet, Grandma pulled in a nice little trout. She ran the stringer through the fish's gills and out through its mouth and tossed it onto the grass nearby. Both my sister and I thought we were getting some nibbles, and we probably were, but Grandma quickly got her hook baited again and this time tossed her line into the pool under an overhanging bank on the far side of the creek. Splat! Instantly, Grandma caught another one.

As we moved upstream to what Grandma thought was another likely spot, she was busy baiting her hook as we walked. It was now light enough that we could see that she was using neither worms nor crickets, but some tiny, winged creature that was barely visible in the early morning light. "Grandma, what are you using for bait?" my sister wanted to know.

"Mayflies. Best trout bait there is. Do you want to try one?" Grandma responded.

Of course Sis wanted to bait her hook with a mayfly, and so did I, but that was much easier said than done. Grandma held the canning jar out and opened the lid just enough for Sis to slide her hand inside and grab a mayfly. She then grasped the tiny, ethereal creature in her fingers and squinting in the dim light, tried, without success, to impale it on her hook.

"There is just one way you can hook a mayfly," Grandma instructed her granddaughter and then demonstrated. "You have to run the hook through the back of its head, right where it joins the body, like this."

I could not see any way that you could run a hook through a creature which appeared to be smaller around than the hook, but Grandma succeeded in baiting my sister's hook for her. "Now slide the sinker further up your line," Grandma instructed. "You want the mayfly to stay at the top of the water. Don't let it sink down into the water like you would a worm."

With more direction from Grandma, Sis soon had caught her first fish of the morning, leaving me, as usual, the one with no success. But Grandma then baited my hook with a mayfly, and, with her guiding me, I tossed the hook into the water at just the place she suggested. In short order, I had caught a little rainbow trout of my own.

As we were fishing, Grandma continued to whisper bits of fishing lore; how to recognize a good fishing spot, how weather and the time of day affect the fishing, and of course, the best bait to use. "It's always best if you can use what the fish are already feeding on," Grandma said, "and that depends on the season. A Mayfly just lives one day, and you can only find them for one or two weeks of the year. But when they are out, mayflies are trout's favorite food." I wondered if all those flat-land sportsmen who had driven in from miles away, and who at that very moment, were down on the Dan River, fishing with their fancy fly rods, creels, and waders, knew all that. I was viewing my grandmother in an entirely new light.

We fished on for over an hour, working our way up the creek and under the stone bridge to where the Blue Ridge Parkway crosses Mayberry Creek, then on up the right branch towards Simon Scott's Tannery, when we reached a point where the rhododendron on the creek bank was almost impassable and getting a line into the creek became very difficult. If Grandma had had enough mayflies, I guess we would have pressed on until we all caught our limit, but even Grandma was not successful in baiting her hook with the transparent little insect more than about half the time. We were about out of mayflies anyway, so Grandma suggested that we had better quit catching fish and go clean the ones we had so she could cook them for breakfast. It had not occurred to me until then, but the moment Grandma mentioned cooking the trout for breakfast, I realized that I was starving! Still, I had caught only two fish.

"Let me try for one more, Grandma," I pleaded. I really wanted to catch at least one fish completely on my own.

Grandma stood patiently by as I baited my hook with an earthworm and my sister loudly complained that I was wasting everyone's time. But I got my hook baited, slid the sinker back down the line, and lowered the line into the water to just above where it cascaded over a large, flat rock. Using the technique I had just learned from Grandma, I let the bait wash over the rock into the pool below. Bam! As soon as the bait washed into the pool, it was nabbed by what I could immediately see was a very large rainbow trout. With Grandma's urging me to not let the fish get any slack, I was able to get it up and onto the bank. Although Grandma thought I should let her remove the flopping fish from the hook, I was insistent that I could to do it all myself. Holding my breath the whole time, I carefully unhooked the struggling creature and did not breathe again until I successfully slid it onto our heavily loaded stringer.

No measurement was necessary. Anyone who looked at the stringer could see that the fish I had just caught was the largest one of all, and it was a fish that I had caught entirely on my own! Sis quickly pointed out that she had caught <u>more</u> fish than I had, but that did not diminish my joy. No. I had caught the largest fish, on a hook I had baited myself, and that made me the winner. As we hiked back to Grandma's house, my eternally competitive sister continued to insist that she was the winning fisherman, but nothing she could have said at that point could have made me feel that I was not the winner of the contest that, until a few moments earlier, I had not even realized was in progress.

"How did you get to be so good at fishing, Grandma?" I later queried, as we sat around the table, feasting on warm corn bread and our freshly caught bounty.

"Lord have mercy, honey, when I was a young'un, if we hadn't known how to fish, we probably would have starved." She began her story once again, and this time I was all ears.

Mayberry Creek

The Winter of Forty-One
Edna Watts

On December 7, 1941, our radio was broken, but a neighbor, who always seemed to know about such things, came by to tell us that the Japanese had bombed Pearl Harbor.

To a six-year-old who had never heard of Pearl Harbor and had barely heard of the Japanese, the immediate meaning of this was not clear. The grownups became quiet and serious; they were also less inclined to make great issues of my childish trespasses.

Once repaired, the radio became the center of all existence. Unfortunately, the repair did not last too long, and our radio was inoperable for much of the war. Tyler Quesinberry was the only person anywhere around Mayberry who could fix radios, and he went off to Newport News to work in a war plant that made radar systems. Typically, the rumor circulated through Meadows of Dan and Mayberry that it was Tyler who had actually invented radar and that the government had actually stolen it from him.

When the radio was working, all horseplay and bickering between my little brother and me had to stop as our parents bent intently over the little RCA to learn whether Gabriel Heatter's sonorous tenor would be announcing whether there was bad news or good news tonight, folks: in those early days of the war, it was mostly bad. The same rule of silence applied to our household when President Roosevelt addressed the nation.

About this time, two new terms entered my vocabulary: *the draft* and *rationing.*

The young men who had formerly picked on me at the general store were now showing up in uniforms, and they no longer had time to waste picking on a kid. They were dignified men now, centers of adult attention, experts whose opinions were valued. Before many months, word would start coming back that one of them, and then another, had been killed in some remote pocket of the world.

I remember being deposited with my grandmother – an experience I usually dreaded, since she often took the occasion to dose me with milk of magnesia, judging that my mother was neglecting this essential health regimen – so that my parents could wait in line for most of a day in the county seat to get ration-stamp books.

They would return grim and complaining. Some of the stamps would never be used, since we grew most of our own food, including meat. But tires, gasoline, sugar, shoes, light bulbs – these were to be worried about.

For growing kids, shoes were a particular problem, although imitation leather synthetics were unrationed and available. Mamma ordered me a pair of saddle oxfords to wear to school. But when they arrived, we found they were made of something similar to cardboard and they only lasted until the first rain.

And the propaganda! What a boon the war must have been for unemployed cartoonists. Posters everywhere: "Loose lips sink ships," "button your lip," " be smart, act dumb." Cartoon caricatures of the "Axis": Hitler, Mussolini, Tojo. I never knew why they picked on Tojo instead of Hirohito. Probably because he was uglier and his name sounded funnier. Goebbels, Hitler's propaganda minister, was caricatured frequently, too. I think now of the irony in the Nazi propaganda minister becoming the icon of hideous cartoons.

In case one was worried about enemy agents infiltrating his neighborhood, an informative article in Life Magazine, illustrated by Milton Caniff, explained how to tell the difference between Japanese and Chinese. The Chinese were illustrated as infinitely more handsome, taller, straighter, smoother. And oh, yes, Japanese had telltale spaces between their toes from wearing thong sandals. In Mayberry, of course, none of us had never seen an individual of either nationality

Old Bugs Bunny and Popeye animated cartoons that are occasionally rerun on Saturday morning television even now are reminders of the extent to which propaganda was directed toward children. It was always "Japs" who emerged from submarines to get pounded by Popeye. Perhaps the Huns looked too much like us to be effective cartoon material or perhaps too many of us had German ancestors.

Band leader Spike Jones had his own effective methods.

"Ven Der Fuehrer says, 'Ve iss der master race,'

We'll go, 'Heil, pffllt! Heil, pffllt!,' right in Der Fuehrer's face!

Now, to love Der Fuehrer is a terrible disgrace,

So we 'Heil, pffllt! Heil, pffilt!,' right in Der Fuehrer's face!"

Joey, the son of a school friend of my mother's, spent summers with us – a convenience for his mother, a delight for me. He learned a lot of things in Jersey City that we country kids were not privy to. Like the Hitler ditty. I had never been allowed to make raspberry noises until he provided me with an acceptable excuse.

It was on my ninth birthday that I learned my father had been drafted. I was sitting in a barber chair in Stuart getting a shingle bob. The draft notice had been kept secret around my house, but when the men in the shop asked Daddy point-blank, he admitted that his number had been picked. I got dizzy.

The night before he left was the first time I had ever seen him cry. We all huddled together on the couch near the wood stove in the living room, my 4-year-old brother and I lying on top of Mama and Daddy, all of us hugging each other, bawling and soggy. Daddy was nearly 33, unable to swim, and was terrified of water. Naturally, he was assigned to the Navy.

My dad's youngest brother was also a sailor, but the one in between had been deferred because he worked at a defense plant. When he, too, got his notice, my grandma invested in a three-star service flag to hang in her window. Uncle Early was waiting for the bus to take him to boot camp when the Presidential order came that no more men over 26 would be inducted; Uncle Early turned around and went home. Grandma's three-star flag was a waste of good money, a fact that I thought she dwelt on a bit too much, given the alternative.

My mother, teaching full time, took on the farm work as well. Daddy had sold three of our cows, leaving just two. Mama milked one cow, I the other. In the dark winter evenings, she would pull on rubber galoshes and wade out into the snow to scatter hay for their feed. Younger brother Aaron fed the pigs and chickens.

Aunt Eileen and her baby moved in with us. Mama's youngest sister was married to an Army captain

stationed in India who had never seen his child. We had a
1937 Dodge and a B-sticker for gas. My aunt could drive;
my mother could not.

Mama never bothered with leg make-up, but my
aunt and my older cousins did. Not only did they
substitute tan paint for the stockings that were no longer
available; they penciled a heavy brown line up the back
of their legs to represent seams, seamless hosiery not
having yet been invented. Long pants were unheard of for
public appearances, and hemlines had risen to an all-time
high for the expedient of saving fabric. There must have
been some very cold legs during those mountain winters.

Our school strove to make itself a military camp.
Everything was geared toward "the war effort." Jack Agee
played *The American Patrol* in the annual piano recital,
to a rousing ovation. The production ended with a chorus
of God *Bless America.* I was dressed as a Red Cross nurse,
and great tears of patriotism streamed down my cheeks as
I sang.

Nothing about "victory gardens" was new but the
name, since everybody there grew his own food anyway.
But the school's spring fund-raising project, which
launched every kid out into the community with a box of
Burpee vegetable seeds to sell, had never before been so
successful. Only now we got rewarded for our successes
with Defense Savings Stamps instead of mechanical
pencils.

The Victory Corps drilled during recess. To join,
one had to sell a $25 War Bond; each additional sale
earned a promotion and an additional, blue-bias-tape
chevron for one's sleeve. I made corporal. Calvin Willis
was the commander; he made major the first week.

When I went out to collect donations for the USO, a neighbor who also happened to be a fundamentalist preacher gave me a stern lecture about all the satanic goings-on in those gov'mint-sponsored hotbeds of sin. I was appalled by his lack of patriotism and my mama was furious.

Because kapok from the Philippines was no longer available, the Navy was using milkweed floss to stuff life vests. Aaron and I filled one burlap sack after another with milkweed pods. Twenty years later milkweed was still nearly extinct from the area.

The scrap-metal drive cleared out the family junkyards as rusty tin stoves, broken axles, sprung hay rakes, and Model-T fenders piled up to form a mountain in the schoolyard. Tin cans, stomped flat and tied in bales, were added. Carl Coggin got his picture in The Enterprise, riding a bicycle towing a *Radio Flyer* wagon piled high with scrap behind. He survived the Second World War only to die on the beach at Incheon, Korea

The arrival of Life Magazine was the major weekly event in our house. Aaron and I fought to be the first to possess it because first claim meant ownership of the full-page Army Air Corps shoulder patch. (It never would have occurred to us to combine our collection.) We would flip past color photos of fly-blown dead soldiers, shuddering and grimacing, looking for that prize. We didn't even *like* the Army; we fell out with neighbors' kids more than once over their insistence that the Army was not a sissy outfit like the Navy. But the Air Corps was undeniably glamorous.

We studied Life's airplane identification silhouettes. Before the war, one plane per month, perhaps, flew over the mountains, everyone turning out to squint at it, but now planes frequently flew over in great formations. A new source for quarrels had arisen. We argued hotly over the identification of every flying object, our only agreement coming when a rare P-38 Lockheed Lightning happened to appear, unmistakable because of its twin fuselages. Nevertheless, we painted our sled to resemble a Flying Tiger, managing somehow to agree on what one looked like.

I savored Life's serialization of Eddie Rickenbacker's *Seven Came Through,* an account of wartime survival in a life raft. One week I had a patched-over infected eye. Mama caught me reading with the good eye and hollered at me roundly, with little effect. I read it anyway, once her back was turned.

Looking back now, I know that my brother was only 2 when the war began, 6 when it ended; but he is perennially frozen in my memory as a 4-year-old with a pinched, worried face. It was during that year that the nightmares came to him, night after night, of Japanese bombings. He once dreamed that he had a pony stabled in the barn and that the Japanese bombed it and killed his pony.

Daddy came home on leave once and surprised Mama in her fourth-grade classroom. She kicked over a chair or two on her way to greet him. The principal gave her the rest of the day off, calling in a substitute; the fourth grade spent the rest of the afternoon doing their impressions of Mrs. Eunice kicking over chairs.

Daddy's next leave was not so happy. Aaron and I had been carrying wood in anticipation of a snowstorm. I got too sick to tote another stick, so sick that my brother's accusations of goldbricking were not enough, for once, to dissuade my mother from packing me off to bed.

The snow came; so did my dad, that night. He woke me up, as he always did; he was squeezing me tightly, but I had to tell him, "Oh, Daddy, I'm so sick," and disengage myself to lie down again. A visit from my aunt the nurse the next morning, followed rather rapidly by the sound of the snow chains on Dr. Thompson's '41 Chevrolet coupe, produced the pronouncement that I had diphtheria. I heard Daddy get into his four-buckle Arctics; I knew from snatches of conversation drifting back that he was going over to the Telephone Central to call and try to get an emergency extension of his leave. I strained when he got back to hear the report: "Shipping out... they won't let me stay."

I recovered, so rapidly, in fact, that one teacher felt compelled to call up the Health Department for assurance that I wasn't contagious. Mama was furious again.

Meanwhile, my dad was on his way to Iwo Jima. The ship he was on shelled the island for weeks, and a kamikaze took the top off the superstructure of his battleship, the *USS New York.* As soon as they finished up at Iwo Jima, they cruised over to Okinawa and did the same thing.

Everyone thought the war was about over, but our radio was out again, so a neighbor had come by to tell us that the Japanese had surrendered. I was churning butter, and my efforts became so energetic that they made the butter form almost immediately. When I shouted the news out the back door to my brother who was feeding the pigs, he danced on top of the pig shed. We both thought our dad would be home in a matter of days.

During the campaign for the Pacific, we had become accustomed to having weeks pass without hearing from Daddy. But now that the war was over, why did we have to endure such a long period of time with no word? We could not have known that his ship was a part of the "obsolete fleet" being assembled for atomic bomb testing at another Pacific island.

Months after the war, I remember finally being awakened by Daddy once again and spotting, first thing, the "ruptured duck" insignia on his Navy blues. I knew what it meant: "You're discharged!" One of the first things he wanted us to know was that if President Roosevelt had lived, the Japanese surrender would have surely been signed on the battleship New York — New York being Roosevelt's home state — instead of the USS Missouri — President Truman's home state.

Mabry's Mill

The Crash

It felt to me as though the whole house shook. When I ran into my mom's bedroom in the middle of the night and told her that an airplane had just crashed, and very close by, she grumpily assured me that I had been dreaming. She hadn't heard a thing and neither had my older sister. But I heard what I heard.

Like so many men we knew in that summer of 1945, my father was away fighting in the war. We knew he had shipped out from San Francisco for some place in the Pacific some three months before and it had been almost two months since we had heard a word. Meanwhile, we were struggling along on the home front, with my mom and my ten year old sister trying to keep the farm together until Dad returned. I was barely six and, other than feeding the chickens and the pigs, very little help.

That particular July Saturday was memorable because Mom had finally gotten someone to mow the waist high grass in our yard with a horse-drawn hay mower. We raked the dried grass into shocks that day with the intention of carrying it out and putting into a stack later. After supper, my sister and I sat out in the yard on a shock of hay to watch the stars come out, and as had become a pretty ordinary occurrence, a formation of military aircraft flew over.

There had been an unusual number of aircraft flying over our Virginia farm for some time now, but we had no way of knowing why or from where they flew. My imagination provided plenty of details, however. After the war, someone who had been in the Air Corps told us that

the planes were mostly flying out of Goldsboro, North
Carolina, to practice bombing runs somewhere over West
Virginia.

"I think those are Jap airplanes," I pessimistically
informed my sister, as we watched the vee formation of
multi-engined aircraft fly over.

"You're nuts," replied Sis, with her usual
diplomatic assessment of my opinions. "Those are
American B-24's. The Japs don't have any airplanes that
even look like that."

"Well, they just don't look like American planes to
me," I lamely countered. But I was relieved because I knew
she was right. She read Life magazine and had memorized
the silhouettes of just about every aircraft involved in the
conflict. I also believe to this day that the Peanuts character
of Lucy was based on my older sister. Anyway, mom called
us in to wash our feet and go to bed, no excuses.

I had no way of knowing what time it was, but I had
heard the rumbling of an airplane's engines for what
seemed a long time before I heard the crash. Airplanes
seldom woke me up, but this one sounded different. At
first, I thought we were being bombed, but then I realized
the plane had crashed and it had to be nearby. I was not
dreaming and Mom and Sis were just plain wrong.

Imagine my feelings of vindication early the next
morning when my Aunt Eileen drove down the drive to our
house and asked, even before she was out of the car, "Did
you hear about the plane crash?" My aunt and her young
daughter were mostly staying with us for the duration, but
they had spent the night with my grandparents, and their
radio worked. They had heard the airplane, and they also
heard on the radio that there was an airplane crash in the

area. Probably due to wartime security restrictions, specific details were not given.

Aunt Eileen was far more adventurous than my mom, and although it would burn precious rationed gasoline, nothing would do but for her to go look for the crash site. And although she implied that we would probably suffer eternal punishment for missing Sunday School, Mom reluctantly agreed to let my sister and me accompany Aunt Eileen on the search.

We had no idea where to begin looking, but as we were preparing to pull out of the drive, a pickup which had its bed filled with a dignified looking party of seven or eight passengers, all seated in straight-backed wooden chairs, drove by. (A pick-up with the bed filled with chairs was a common method of dealing with the war-time transportation shortage in rural areas of the South.) "Follow that pickup," my sister instructed. "They must be headed for the plane crash."

The increase in the number of vehicles headed in the same direction as the pickup reinforced everyone's opinion but mine that we were on the right track, but I knew we were much too far from home. Then we, along with a number of others, pulled into the parking lot of The Maple Shade Primitive Baptist Church, just in time for the Invocation of the Annual Primitive Baptist Association and Dinner on the Grounds. The driver of the pickup we had followed knew, however, where the crash had occurred; about four miles back in the direction from which we had just come, right behind Mabry's Mill and about a half-mile north of our house. His wife also warmly invited us to join the family for the dinner on the grounds, assuring us that they had plenty of food for everyone. But we could not be distracted from the search.

The crash site, which was located without further incident, certainly did not match up to what I had imagined. There were no pillars of smoke or roiling blazes, no crater in the earth and no path blasted through shattered trees. There were just a lot of big pieces of shiny metal scattered all over a large field. There was a rope stretched all around the site, with a few park rangers and deputies posted here and there. No one said a word, however, when I grabbed a Spam can-sized aluminum object lying at the edge of the field outside the ropes and stuffed it in my shirt.

Neighbors who preceded us to the site were more than happy to provide us with details: The crash had occurred about 3:00 am. The pilot and crew were training for night flying when they somehow became separated from their squadron, lost radio contact, and became lost. They were flying in a search pattern looking for their base, some two hundred miles away, when they ran low on fuel and everyone bailed out. The pilot jumped last, just before the plane crashed, and he was apparently the only casualty. Bailing out from such a low altitude, he had broken his leg upon landing in a neighbor's patch of woods. The family heard the pilot's cries for help, extracted him from the woods, and had summoned an ambulance to take him to the nearest hospital, some twenty miles away.

I overheard the neighbor's teen-age daughter telling all about the rescue of the pilot and how they cared for him in their home until the ambulance arrived. The girl also quietly confided to my sister that the pilot had said that she could keep his parachute. Later, my sister embellished the story considerably, declaring that the daughter and the pilot had fallen hopelessly in love. Sis was sure that the pilot would return after the war to claim the girl who had helped rescue him and that they would be married, with the daughter wearing a wedding dress made from the white parachute he had given her.

Even at the age of six, I thought that was the silliest crock of romantic nonsense I could imagine. The pilot did not return to claim the neighbor's daughter or his parachute. But I know it all was not a dream, because even as I write this, the aircraft fuel filter that I pilfered from the crash site, now functioning as a paperweight, sits on the desk in front of me.

The Telephone Exchange

One day in the summer of 1946, an employee of the Stuart-Laurel Fork Telephone Company came into our home and screwed a hand-cranked wooden contraption that looked like a troll onto the wall of our living room. With the pair of brass bells as eyes, the transmitter on the end of a stalk extending from the center of the box resembling a nose, and a shelf extending like a protruding upper lip right below the transmitter, it really did look like a scary face to a small child. The generator crank protruding from the box on the right side and the receiver hanging from the left made up the lop-sided ears which completed the monster. This was our first telephone.

My parents were married in 1933, right in the most severe year of The Great Depression, but with some help from my grandfather, they were able to purchase a small, swampy farm. The farm came with a large and somewhat dilapidated old farm house with no telephone or electricity. They got electricity in just a few years, but they couldn't yet afford a telephone. By the time they could, World War II was underway and the installation of telephones was suspended for the duration. Besides, if there was an emergency, one only had to walk a half-mile to the general store to make a call.

At the time of the installation, I was just tall enough to read the small brass plaque on the base of the telephone. It stated that the model of Western Electric Telephone on our wall was patented in 1898. I later learned that it was actually manufactured around 1915, and that the owners of the Stuart-Laurel Fork Telephone Company obtained their equipment by purchasing the out-of-date discards of urban telephone systems which were being updated.

To make a call on a "troll" telephone, the equivalent of a telephone number had to be cranked out in a sort of Morse Code using the handle that protruded from the right side of the box. The twelve subscribers on our party line could call each other directly, and our "ring" was a short-ring, a long-ring, and a short-ring. Calls to someone on another line or long-distance had to be routed through Central. The switch board operator at Central was summoned by grinding out two long rings, usually multiple times.

I stayed with some cousins in Pueblo, Colorado for a time in 1948. My strongest memory, other than the water being almost undrinkable, was a telephone system on which, when you picked up the receiver, a nasal voice would inquire "*Number Please?*" It was all very strange; how did the voice know that I needed a number? It too was a party line, but with only five subscribers. Those telephones were the tall, skinny "candlestick" models like you might see used in 1940's movies or on the Andy Griffith Show.

On our phone system, there were several nosy neighbors who would listen in on everyone's calls. Sometimes so many would listen in that the system could not power all of the receivers connected into the line and the incoming voice would become inaudible. Then you would have to ask for some people listening in to please hang up. That failing, one might be forced to attach specific names to the request. Or, you could respond like one of our neighbors. He would just yell into the transmitter, "Would some of you busy-bodies get off the line?"

In my teen years, the switchboard would sometimes be operated by a girl who was a classmate of mine. I found out that she was listening in whenever I called the young lady whom I considered to be my girlfriend at the time, and then telling everything we said to her giggly friends at school. I was furious about it then, but I later decided it was probably all because she kind of liked me.

In the late 1950's, Lee Telephone Company bought out the Stuart-Laurel Fork Telephone Company and installed a dial system. The telephones were all made of hefty black Bakelite and had rotary dials. It was great being on a party line with only four subscribers. Your telephone no longer rang when other phones on your line were being called,   but you still had to listen in before you dialed to keep from interrupting others' conversations. As an added convenience, Dad connected an extra long line to our one telephone so that someone wanting to converse in private could carry the telephone into the bathroom.

In the 60's, the availability of modern telephone designs and features exploded. Magazine and television ads told us that multiple phones, colored phones, and "touch-tone dialing" were now essential, all at an extra cost, of course. When we had the telephone service installed in our first home, my wife and I discovered that the luxury of an avocado colored telephone on the kitchen wall would cost an extra $2.50 per month. When visiting my parents back in Virginia, I would observe that their one telephone was the same old black Bakelite rotary dial model from the fifties.   Their party-line system was dispensed with sometime in that decade, but my father, a true child of the Depression, didn't think the private-line convenience was worth the slight increase in the telephone bill.

In 1968, the courts ruled that AT&T could not require its customers to use only those telephones manufactured or licensed by its subsidiary, Western Electric. By the 70's, people were buying smaller, cheaper telephones from Radio Shack and installing the second and third telephones themselves. Whenever you called Southern Bell with a service problem, the service representative always intimated that any non-Western Electric telephones you might be using were probably the problem. They also started trying to sell you wire insurance.

Sometime in the 80's, the rotary dial on my parent's thirty year-old telephone began sticking. Dad sprayed it with WD-40, and when that failed to solve the problem, Mom and Dad agreed to let me find them a new telephone. I bought them a fancy new touch-tone telephone from K-Mart which worked perfectly, but it was small and light and they never liked it much. There was just something fundamentally wrong with a telephone that produced musical tones.

Even in the 90's, when my dad was in a retirement home and could only see to dial a telephone with an extra-large illuminated key pad, he longed for his old rotary dial. We all must long for them, come to think of it, since we still talk about "dialing" a number, a term which specifically refers to the action of rotating a dial to generate the code which connects one telephone with another. It is similar to hearing young people who have never seen a "troll" telephone talk about "hanging-up" their cell phones to end the conversation. The term "hang-up the phone" originally referred to the act of hanging the receiver from the bracket on the side of the troll, the weight of the receiver opening the switch and disconnecting the phone.

Writing about telephones has prompted me to take an inventory. Together, my wife and I currently own seven or eight functioning telephones, making me wonder if we have lost our minds. The change in peoples' lives and the convenience provided by multiple, mobile, cellular, and smart telephones is miniscule when compared to the change and convenience created by the introduction of that first single telephone in the home. When I look back on the advent of twentieth century technology and the effect it has had on our lives, I am led to the conclusion that almost all of the advances in technology which have resulted in truly significant improvements in the quality of our lives were available to Ozzie and Harriet in 1950. If I have to explain who Ozzie and Harriet were, then you would probably disagree.

Summertime in Paradise

Mayberry Creek runs for a distance of more than half a mile through what was once my grandparent's farm. One of the creek's origins is a spring on the southern slope of Hurricane Knob, from which it cascades down through the wooded hollow, joined along the way by contributing springs and branches, its journey only temporarily impeded by the two fish ponds constructed in its path. Deep in the woods just west of the Blue Ridge Parkway, the southern tributary is joined by a heavily polluted stream of similar size which originates near a diary farm on the northern slope of Hurricane Knob. As the combined stream emerges from the woods, it is forced to make a sharp s-turn, following the new path created for it by the construction of the Parkway. It then obediently slows to a calm pool, flowing leisurely beneath the beautiful stone bridge constructed especially for it, then accelerating as it meanders across the meadow towards Mayberry Road. The stream cascades vigorously into the culvert and is carried under Mayberry Road, changing to a calming babble as it flows across the lower pasture. Just before reaching the culvert under Mayberry Creek Road, once the southern terminus of Grandpa's farm, it narrows again and tumbles over a rock ledge and chicanes erratically down a narrow ravine before disappearing under the road.

Grandma and Grandpa's tall, white house still stands there, right next to where the Mayberry Road crosses Mayberry Creek. Both the house and the creek seem so much smaller to me now than they were back then.

On most summer Sunday afternoons our families would gather at my grandparents' house in Mayberry for dinner, after which, the cousins would organize themselves into a scouting party and the adventures would begin. As we would gather in the side yard of the house, the first order of business was simply, in which direction should we proceed? We made interesting discoveries in any direction our explorations might take us. In the summer though, no matter what the direction of our initial foray, by late in the afternoon we would end up at the creek.

A summertime obsession of some of us cousins was to dam up Mayberry Creek sufficiently to create a swimming hole. Many hot summer Sundays saw an amazing effort expended in attempting to build a rock and sod dam across the creek, and if a parent objected to our project on the premise that our project might flood the meadow, Grandma would come to our defense. "Oh, don't worry about that," she would reassure them. "The first big rain that comes, that dam will be gone." And she was right. We tried several likely locations, but no single Sunday afternoon ever provided sufficient time to completely dam up the creek, and by the time we resumed our efforts, a week or two later, the beginnings of our previous dam would have always washed away.

The crew of explorers was usually, but not always, made up of a gaggle of boy cousins of which I was about the median age. There were Danny, Buddy, and Roy, who were two, three, and four years younger than me, respectively, and then Richard and Fred, both two years older than me. The two older of the cousins would often abandon the group pretty early because Fred would have to go home to do farm chores and Richard would often accompany him, intimating that the interests of us younger cousins were just too childish for one of his wisdom and maturity. Sometimes, especially if cousins from Colorado or Iowa were visiting back east, a number of girl cousins might accompany the expeditions, at least until we ended up at the creek. A really important excursion, such as a chinquapin picking, might attract a dozen cousins.

Sometimes our forays were directed for us; from June through August our excursions were often initiated by Grandma handing out buckets and telling us to go see if there were any Yellow Transparent or Virginia Beauty or Milam or whatever apples had a possibility of being ripe at that particular time. This was definitely not a burdensome task; any excuse to hike up into the orchard and climb apple trees was welcomed, with the only precaution being to keep away from Grandpa's bee hives. Thirty years after my grandparents passed away, I still had people asking me if Grandma's big old Yellow Transparent apple tree near the Parkway was still standing. I would have to tell them no, that the century old tree, already ailing, was finished off by Hurricane Hugo.

For a few years after electric power came to Mayberry, Grandma's wash house was a favorite stop. As soon as electric power became available, the noisy gasoline engine on Grandma's Maytag washing machine was replaced with a quiet, reliable electric motor, but the old two-stroke gasoline engine with a kick starter and a huge aluminum flywheel languished in the corner of the wash house for years. For a time, it was a real contest of kid against machine to see if we could tromp on the starter pedal and get it to fire. The few times it actually started, it would bounce around on the wash house floor, generating billows of smoke and making a deafening racket, until we could get to the fuel valve and shut it down. This entertainment all ended after there was no more fuel in the engine tank and Grandpa had confiscated the gasoline can.

One of our favorite places to visit was Grandpa's power dam, which extended across Mayberry Creek down at the lower end of the farm, near the cascade at the Cold Spring Road. Sometime in the mid-nineteen thirties, Grandpa and his son in law, Neal Stanley, had dammed up the creek at the upper end of the cascade and built a flume to divert water to a small turbine. The turbine was connected to a Homelite Electric Power Generator located inside a little shack at the lower end of the cascade.

I can barely recall when the Power System was operational, but one thing I clearly remember is that when electricity was needed, the first step was to open the gate in the dam that allowed water into the flume. This was accomplished by going out into the yard to crank a windlass and wind in a cable strung through pulleys suspended from tall poles. The cable ran all the way from Grandpa's house to the dam, a distance of a quarter of a mile.

The system never seemed to work very well, even when operating at its best. It generated only enough electricity to power a few dim bulbs, priority being given to one light in the barn for milking and one each in the kitchen and the dining room at dinner time. Power for the Silvertone Radio during Gabriel Heatter's News Report was also given a high priority. I can well remember my Aunt Eileen's complaints about the system being insufficient to power her electric iron, even if every other electrical device in the house was turned off.

Years later, I made a calculation of how much power the Homelite plant could have theoretically produced by the water flowing from the top of the seven-foot high dam across Mayberry Creek and came up with less than one kilowatt. Calculating the power generated was a moot exercise anyway, since just a few years after the dam was built, the flume was washed away in a heavy rain storm and the pond was filled with silt. But long after it was no longer useful for generating power, the dam across Mayberry Creek continued to be a wonderful place for kids to visit. The water pouring over the top of the dam made a lot of exciting noise, and we could still pull on the cable and raise the gate that once fed the missing flume to release more water and make it even louder. And, although the little powerhouse was kept locked for the express purpose of keeping curious kids out, we could look through the one small window and wonder over the disused generator and marvel at the wires and gauges, about whose function we had not a clue.

Once, Uncle Bud came down when we were playing around the "power house," to see what we were up to. He came to the conclusion that if a kid crawled under the power house and turned the turbine while kids above the powerhouse were fiddling with wires, an electrocution could result. All exposed wires wire quickly disconnected to eliminate the danger, but Uncle Neal later explained that it was a twenty four volt power system, so a mild shock would have been the worst that could have happened. At least now we knew why Aunt Eileen's 110 volt iron wouldn't heat up.

At the time of my earliest recollections, the pasture beside the creek above the dam was the domain of Grandpa's two retired mules, Dan and Rhody. The mules would sometimes come loping up toward us when we would go inside the fence that surrounded the pasture. We were afraid of them, but not frightened enough to keep out.

But one Sunday, as we were crossing the pasture, the mules came galloping up especially aggressively and we sought refuge in an old farm wagon parked in the field. The mules stood guard by the wagon for what seemed like hours, as we waited and wailed for some adult to please come and rescue us. The aunts and uncles could see our predicament from the front porch of Grandpa's house, but they were having too much fun at our expense for anyone to consider helping us out. After Grandpa finally walked down to the pasture and shooed the mules away, he suggested that whenever we encroached on the mules' domain that maybe we should carry a peace offering in the form of handfuls of feed. We followed his advice and soon learned that the mules were, in fact, quite docile. The only reason they pursued us in the first place in the hope that we had something for them to eat.

One of the greatest adventures of all would happen when our oldest cousin, Coy Lee, would hitch up the mules to Grandpa's surrey and take us on rides up and down the Mayberry Road. One Sunday, he actually took some of the older cousins to the Talbot Reservoir and then to a lookout point from which the Pinnacles of the Dan could be viewed. We younger cousins were not allowed on that trip, though, and were inadequately compensated by a short ride up Mayberry Road to the Presbyterian Church and back.

One Sunday afternoon, a group of us cousins emigrated all the way up the lane to the top of Hurricane Knob. There is a point there where Patrick, Floyd, and Carroll Counties all come together, with the corner of Floyd County squeezed into a narrow triangle. The point of intersection of the three counties was clearly marked, and since the water shed (the Eastern Continental Divide, actually, and also the county line) could sort of be discerned, older Cousins Jimmie and Fred Yeatts claimed to be able to tell the locations of the county lines. They laid down two sticks to form an angle, and we all took turns jumping across the sticks representing the county boundaries. I don't recall being too impressed by the exercise at the time, but looking back from the perspective of sixty years, "the day we jumped across Floyd County" seems pretty special.

If we were in Mayberry on a day other than a Sunday, the old Mayberry Store, operated by our Uncle Coy, was the major attraction. (Nothing was open on Sunday in Patrick County in those days except the churches.) Sometimes, Grandma would give us eggs to exchange for Nehi Sodas or chocolate drops, and sometimes Uncle Coy would give us bubble gum, just to aggravate our mothers, all of whom were highly vocal about how much they despised the stuff. A little further east and up the road from the store were Mayberry Presbyterian Church, which then was never locked, and the abandoned Mayberry School building, which was dangerously dilapidated, making it an even more attractive site for exploration. I recall being paddled after my dad caught me on the rickety porch of the old school, a place I had been expressly forbidden to go. But there was a sassafras tree growing through the porch floor, and that absolutely demanded a close inspection.

Grandpa's garage, which stood at the intersection of the lane and Mayberry Road, held his 1940 Pontiac, the surrey, and his mail buggy. If we kids could get into the garage, the big problem then was to decide which vehicle each of us would pretend to drive. We would sometimes return from our pretend excursions in the buggy and surrey absolute filthy and in serious trouble with our mothers.

An odd room tacked onto the side of the garage had one wall filled with pigeon holes. It had been Grandpa's mail sorting room after Mayberry Post Office closed and he became a Mail Carrier for the Meadows of Dan Post Office. Some of the pigeon holes still carried names of local RFD patrons.

Perhaps the most mysterious of the Mayberry sites that we so loved to explore was "The Tobe Place." If we followed the lane that ran from the old garage at Mayberry Road, on past our grandparents' house and the assorted out buildings, we would soon come to the stone bridge which allowed the narrow lane and Mayberry Creek to pass, side by side, under the Blue Ridge Parkway. Every kid with whom I have ever walked under that bridge, from then until now, has insisted on stopping and shouting, to listen to the echo. After the lane emerged from under the bridge, there was a gate known to the family as "the milking gap." From there the lane traversed a small pasture and ran into a tunnel of rhododendron that merged into a patch of woods. Within the rhododendron tunnel, there were drawbars which had to be lowered or climbed, and a creek that had to either be jumped or crossed on stepping stones.

Upon emerging from the woods, we would find ourselves at the "Tobe Place," first an old barn surrounded by an open field, and at the far side of the field, in a small orchard, stood a little house with a front porch and two front doors. Others had apparently lived there since Uncle Tobe had left, but no one ever lived there when we were kids, and the house was always locked. But we could thump up the steps onto the front porch and peer in through the windows. There was really nothing much to see on the inside; just walls covered with peeling wallpaper and a small cook stove connected to the chimney by a collapsed stove pipe, but it did seem rather eerie.

Who "Tobe" was, why this was his place, and why no one was ever there was a mystery to us for a long time. Our parents finally must have told us that "Tobe" was Charles Tobias Yeatts, Grandpa's younger brother. He and his family had moved to Montana many years ago, but he had died and all of his family stayed Out West. The only member of Tobe's family who would ever come back to visit was Cousin Roy, who would bring his family back east to visit "Uncle Dump and Aunt Edny" every few years.

For us cousins, once "Tobe" had something of an identity, he became "Uncle Tobe" to us, but there remained so many unanswered questions that our Uncle Tobe continued as an elusive and mysterious figure. I have no idea what he looked like – I never even saw a picture of him – but I always assumed that anyone named "Tobe" would be rather short and rotund and would wear a wide-brimmed felt hat. As we got older and began to pay more attention to the conversations of our parents and aunts and uncles, we learned more about the stories of the several members ours family who had emigrated Out West, and there are many of those tales that are worth repeating.

The Parkway Bridge circa 1938

AH-OOO-GAH!

The second I heard the footsteps on the porch, I could tell it was my father and that he was really mad about something. The back porch of our old farmhouse was badly weathered, with loose and missing boards here and there. Most folks entering our home through the back door would carefully pick their way up the back steps and across the hazards of the deteriorating porch floor, but if my dad was in a hurry or upset about something, he would come in the back way, thundering across the porch, holes and loose boards be damned.

I opened the kitchen door just ahead of Dad's arrival and stepped back, assuming he would come hustling through the door with his arms filled with the groceries he had gone into town to buy, but his hands were empty. Instead of clutching groceries, they were clenched at his sides and his face was an angry red. His eyes narrowed as he loomed over me, backing me across the kitchen before addressing me in a controlled but threatening voice. "You have five damn minutes to get that contraption off my car, mister – or you will never drive it again."

Oh crap! How did I forget? I was going to switch the wiring back before Dad had a chance to drive the car, and I just plain forgot. Dad started using "mister" when he was in service, and whenever he called me "mister," I knew I was in big trouble.

I had been driving for only a few months, and just recently had my folks decided that possibly I was sufficiently trustworthy to take a girl out on a date. That's assuming that I could find a girl who was both willing to go out with me and whose parents also deemed me trustworthy enough for her to go. The girl of my dreams at the time was all gaga over a senior who drove a hot '55 Ford Victoria Tudor and I, understandably attributed my rejection to the fact that our 1953 four door Chevrolet Biscayne was just too dismally uncool.

My many efforts to upgrade the image of the old four-door Chevy were unfailingly stymied by my father's intolerance of any accessory which might possibly be remotely connected to what he contemptuously referred to as "hot-rodding." I spent many late night hours perusing the J.C. Whitney Auto Accessory catalog, searching in vain for add-on items which might spiff-up the old Chevy and still pass my father's muster. The fake dual exhaust pipes, which cost me four weeks' allowance to buy and countless hours to install, had to be removed immediately upon being noticed by my dad. The white porta-walls, installed to cover up the Chevy's uncool black-wall tires suffered a similar fate. The steering knob (also known as a "J. C. Whitney necking knob") which I optimistically installed on the steering wheel of the car was summarily declared by my dad to be "unsafe." Just why and for whom it was unsafe was never made clear. The knob did end up being put to good use on the steering wheel of our old farm tractor, a machine which required a substantial manly effort to guide.

By the standards of that time and place, we were not an awfully poor family, but the experience of The Great Depression was forever imbedded in my father's psyche. We would have had it pretty rough living on what little Dad made by working himself silly running our small farm, but he also held down a full-time job below the mountain. Although his day job did not really depend on political patronage, Dad always liked to keep on the good side of the local political somebodies, just in case.

My father and a couple of our neighbors car-pooled to work, and since my mother did not drive, the car sat at home, mostly unused, for two weeks out of three. When I first suggested that perhaps I could drive the car to run errands and such after school on those weeks that the car sat at home, Dad accused me, in his typical jargon, of wanting to "run around all over the country." I continued to press the point, insisting that I would pay for the gas, tires, insurance and all other expenses associated with my use of the car. Even my dad finally realized that the three and a half dollars I was paid each week for helping on the farm would not exactly give me free rein to "run around all over the country." I think the clincher was when I convinced him that if I could drive the car, I could pick up items such as cow feed and salt blocks at the Southern States Coop and save him some time and effort. I also promised that I would always get home early and have the milking underway by the time he got home. He relented with one strong stipulation: No hauling other kids around all over the country. Dad was – wisely, I now realize – unwilling to assume that liability.

This was all taking place late in the spring of my junior year, with the school year almost to an end, the baseball season over, and all us guys at school getting pretty slack. We were hanging around after school one day, when one of my friends mentioned that his grandpa's Model-A Ford truck had finally died and had been hauled away to Blondie Pilson's Junkyard, the point being that he had rescued the *Klaxon* from off the old truck before it was hauled away, and he could be persuaded to part with this treasure, if the price was right.

The "Klaxon" was one of many examples of early twentieth century products which became so well-known that their brand names became the terms commonly used to refer to all such devices, like some folks would call any kind of refrigerator a "Frigidare, or use the name "Kodak" for any kind of camera. In the 1920's, several automobile manufacturers equipped their cars with a horn similar to those manufactured by the company that made warning devices for ambulances, diving horns for submarines, and emergency alarms for schools and factories. The name embossed on all of these products was "KLAXON," the Greek word for "shriek."

A more common name by which the automobile Klaxon and its many imitators were known was the "AHOOGAH horn," or sometimes just plain "Oogah-horn." It is still pretty much known by this name because, "AH-OO-GAH" is the sound it makes. One can produce a respectable imitation of a Klaxon by taking a deep breath and saying a loud "aaaah" while performing a personal Heimlich maneuver. A light tap or a heavy push on the horn button of a car equipped with a Klaxon has pretty much the same effect. The emission of an ear-splitting AH-OOO-GAH! (Cheap plastic versions of the "Aoogah Horn" are still available today for a modest price from importers such as Harbor Freight, but the sound these make is a pathetic belch compared to the real thing. I also recently discovered that Klaxon is still in business, as a manufacturer of air horns for hockey fans and hikers in bear country.)

In the brief bidding war which erupted over the available Klaxon, I was arguably the winner. It seemed to me at the time that the ah-oo-gah horn might just be the touch that would elevate my dad's old four door Chevrolet

Biscayne from the dismal depths of the intolerably uncool, up and into the domain of the just-slightly-cool. That Friday, five of my hard-earned dollars were exchanged for a thirty-year-old Klaxon in superb condition. After class, I drove the car into the school's vocational-agriculture shop, and with a little help from my friends and a lot of advice from the Vo-Ag teacher, the horn was installed.

The teacher patiently explained the proper installation of an accessory horn on an automobile: The original equipment horn circuit should be left intact, and the accessory horn should be connected in a separate circuit and activated by an accessory horn button. Of course, I did not have an accessory horn button, so we just disconnected the original equipment car horn and connected the Klaxon in its place. There was one minor problem with this quick and easy installation, however. The electrical relay on the old Klaxon did not function properly, and in this particular installation, the operation of the Klaxon required two taps on the horn button: One tap to start the Klaxon blowing, and a second tap – or possibly a third or a fourth – to shut it off. But once the technique was mastered, it worked just fine.

Since its mounting bracket was missing, the horn was securely attached to the inside of the car's grill, just in front of the radiator, with several turns of bailing wire. This method of attachment had the happy affect of causing the Klaxon to vibrate against the metal grill, amplifying its shriek by many decibels. My friends and I were having a great time ahoogahing the old Chevy around the school parking lot, until the assistant principal came striding angrily out of the school building and threatened us all with bodily harm if he heard one more ahoogah. I then departed from the school grounds, and after obligatory side trips to ahoogah the general store, the filling station, and the home of a girl I intended to ask out soon, I drove straight home. By that time running seriously late, I quickly got busy with the farm chores and forgot all about changing the circuit back to the original horn. From that afternoon until Dad's return from his trip to town, I completely forgot that the car was now equipped with a Klaxon of exceptional virtuosity.

Dad never shared the gory details of his trip to town that Saturday and I knew better than to ask, but some stories I heard later gave me a pretty good idea of what must have happened. Whenever my dad had a little spare time, he liked to spend it gossiping with his "court house buddies." Most Saturday mornings, when he would drive into town to buy farm supplies and major groceries, he would also spend time schmoozing with his friends around the court house, discussing important stuff like elections and baseball.

In my mind I can see him now, in his going-to-town starched white shirt, propping up the roof of the old Chevy with his left arm, queued up in the Saturday morning traffic in front of the courthouse. He apparently spotted someone crossing the street with whom he particularly wanted to talk. In the second and third hand versions of the story relayed to me, it was the Commonwealth's Attorney, or the County Treasurer, somebody really important like that. Whomever it was, to attract the bigwig's attention he beeped the horn, and as you must know, the beep came out from under the hood of the car as a deafening and protracted **AH-OOOO-GAH!** Witnesses reported that he had to get out of the car and open the hood to disconnect the horn from the battery before he finally got it to shut off.

As I nervously removed the Klaxon from the car, with my dad leaning impatiently over my shoulder, I recalled the fate of the rejected steering knob, and thought that maybe the tractor could use a good horn. But as soon as I lifted the thing out from under the car hood, Dad grabbed it from me and hustled around the barn with it. I never saw it again and I figured, mad as he was, he probably buried it in the manure pile or threw it into the creek.

A couple of weeks later, as Dad was catching me up on my allowance, I found that I had been given an extra couple of dollars. When I pointed out the excess, Dad responded with a proud smile. "Oh, it's all yours," he insisted. "That extra is the two dollars they gave me for that dad-blamed oogah-horn over at Blondie Pilson's Junkyard."

The Stockman

There were two basic criteria that strongly influenced whether Grandpa thought a man was or was not worth a damn; how early did he get up in the morning and did he keep his pocket knife sharp? My father, one of my grandfather's six sons-in-law, was not found wanting in either judgment, but his ever-sharp pocket knife lay unused, on the top of the dresser right beside his keys, throughout the last years of World War II.

On a few occasions, and with explicit permission and close supervision from Mom, I was allowed to use my dad's pocket knife for some worthy purpose. But I was supposed to never open the little blade, the one blade which was kept especially sharp. The one time I was using the knife without supervision, I disobeyed and used the sharp little blade. Naturally, I cut my finger. Then I compounded the sin by lying about which blade I was using when the accident occurred.

When Dad came home after the war, he brought me an official "U.S. Navy" pocket knife for my very own. He made no special claims about it, but the knife did have "Official U.S. Navy" embossed into the genuine celluloid imitation bone handles. I later learned from one of my Dads friends who had also been in the Navy what I had already begun to suspect. It was not an official U.S. Navy knife; the United States Navy did not issue pocket knives, but that really did not matter to me. Although the blades could not be given an edge sharp enough to cut butter, one blade was a combination bottle opener and screwdriver, and that knife remained my pride and joy until it wore a hole in the pocket of my dungarees and disappeared.

When I was a child, every male over the age of eight whom I knew carried a pocket knife most of the time. Putting my knife in my pocket was as much a part of getting ready for school as pulling on my socks. Bringing a knife to school will get a kid arrested nowadays, but all the guys back then thought they needed pocket knives for lots of practical purposes, none of which were related to violence. The worn out pencil sharpeners in our school ate pencils and broke lead, so how else was a guy supposed to sharpen his own pencil and that of a girl who might seek his assistance?

My dad's knife that I remember so well was a *Case* brand stock knife. What defines a knife as a "stock" knife, I learned at some point in my life, is the three special blades: the sheepsfoot, the clip, and the spey blade. Each is designed for, but not limited to, a specific purpose. The clip blade is the long slender, curved blade with a sharp point, functionally very different than the sheepsfoot blade, with its straight edge and blunt end. The sharpened edge of the spey blade is slightly curved, with its rounded tip sharpened all of the way to the back edge of the blade. The Case brand of pocket knife was considered to be one of good quality at the time, but Dad somehow broke the tip off the clip blade, and continual heavy use eventually caused one of the bone handles to become loose. If epoxy glue had been available back then, I am sure my dad could have repaired it. He expended considerable effort in an attempt to reset the rivets and tighten the handle, but without success. In desperation, he applied a large glob of Duco Household Cement, which held the loose handle in place for about one day, whereupon my frustrated dad just said the heck with it and pried the loose handle all of the way off.

A few weeks before Christmas that year, Mom gave me five dollars and told me to buy Dad a new pocket knife. That was a lot of responsibility for a ten year old, but I was up to the challenge. I really did know quite a bit about pocket knives, including how to use a magnet to test the quality of the steel in the blades. I was able to purchase a Schrade Stockman, one with the requisite three blades, at Midkiff's Hardware in Mt. Airy for exactly five dollars. The fifteen cents North Carolina sales tax I happily paid from my own pocket.

On Christmas Morning, Dad made a big deal over how much he appreciated the knife, and I think he really was pleased, but he continued to carry the Case Knife with the missing handle everyday during the week. The new Schrade Stockman became his Sunday dress-up pocket knife, but all during the week, it lay unused on the top of the dresser.

For my dad, and working people like him, the pocket knife was truly a tool for all seasons. In the winter it was used to shave kindling for starting fires, to graft apple trees, and to open Christmas parcels from Sears and Roebuck. In the spring it was used to cut up seed potatoes and to castrate shoats. In the summer it trimmed bean poles and fitted new tool handles. In the fall, it clipped lengths of fodder twine for tying shocks of corn, peeled apples, and scraped the bristles from scalded hog carcasses. Year round it drilled holes in belts and harnesses, opened feed and fertilizer sacks, and stripped the insulation from wires for electrical connections. Sometimes, on a spring Sunday, if the kids were being good, it was used to make willow whistles or alder pop guns. All of this was happening years before the popular Swiss Army Knife which, I suspect, is still not available with a spey blade.

The men of my extended family were mostly observant of the Sabbath, but that did not mean that the day had to be entirely unproductive. As they would sit around on the front porch after Sunday dinner at Grandma's, my dad and my uncles would sometimes use the relaxing time as an opportunity to hone their pocket knives. One of them might have a small whetstone in his pocket, but if one was not handy, a leather shoe sole could be used to sharpen the knife blades with surprising effectiveness. Whenever my dad was sharpening his Schrade Stockman in the presence of his brothers-in-law, at some point he would always hold the knife up for display and proudly announce, "My boy gave me this knife for Christmas one year. Best knife I ever owned."

Decades later, after Dad had passed away and I was removing his possessions from the retirement home where he spent his last years, the manager of the facility handed me a plastic box containing personal objects which had been put away for safe keeping. There, along with his wallet, his watch, and his Masonic ring, was his Case everyday pocket knife, the one with the missing handle. I was overwhelmed as my mind was flooded with images of the strong, work-worn hands which wielded that basic tool with such care and precision.

I used to heartily agree with comedian George Carlin when he would say something to the effect that "our possessions are just stuff, and stuff is really not worth all that much." But in among all my worthless stuff, one possession which I consider to be a genuine treasure is my father's pocket knife, the one with the missing handle.

Mayberry Meadow

Holsteins and Me

"Blamed groun' hogs!" Uncle Neal cussed and flailed at the steering wheel as the front tire thudded into the deep hole hidden by grass. The old truck careened precariously around the hillside as my elderly and arthritic uncle enthusiastically chauffeured me over his mountain farm, land of which he was extremely proud and part of which I was hoping to buy.

At the end of the tour Uncle Neal explained to me how this tract of family land, should he decide to sell it, would come with several caveats: The family cemetery must be maintained, the land must never be subdivided or sold to anyone outside the family, and Flynn, a grand nephew of Uncle Neal's, could continue pasturing his cattle there. He correctly assumed that my wife and I wanted the land for a retirement home in the mountains. He commented on how it would please him mightily if we built in the edge of the woods at the top of the hill, the site that he and Aunt Vera had once chosen for their dream home that was never built.

Once I had assured Uncle Neal that he could rely on my stewardship of what was once a part of my grandfather's farm, he agreed to sell, right then and there. Neal's wife, Aunt Vera, was not so pleased, convinced as she was that the caveats were unenforceable and that developers were always salivating over scenic land accessible from the Blue Ridge Parkway. She even implied that maybe I was in cahoots with one of them.

Probably, she hoped the land would be bought by Flynn, the real farmer in the family, although I doubted that he had made them a serious offer. Probably, Flynn was already farming as much land as he could manage. At the time I feared that Uncle Neal might be selling because he thought that he might not be around much longer, and in less than a year he was gone. Aunt Vera, however, continued to live in their home at the foot of the hill, forever vigilant to insure that all promises were kept.

The cattle would be no problem for me, I thought. I grew up on a little farm myself. But the cattle that I recalled from the farm of my youth were small and calm, highly domesticated Jerseys. The herd that I found grazing on our newly acquired hillside were modern Holsteins, black and white behemoths. This towering collection of adolescent heifers and steers sported an average weight of over a thousand pounds each, and my first encounter with Holstein eccentricity occurred before we ever started building our cabin.

Not long after we got the place, my wife and I decided to do some exploring. When we drove across the field there was not a cow in sight, so we naively left the car in the field and walked up the hill and into the woods. We returned about an hour later to find our car surrounded by Holstein cattle, all furiously engaged in giving the vehicle a thorough licking.

Now, getting your car slurped on by cows may not sound too serious, but bovine saliva is a sticky, translucent substance, permeated with pieces of partially digested forage. Once it has dried, removal requires soap and water and a lot of elbow grease. In this case, the critters had eaten the windshield wiper blades in the process of giving the windshield a thorough coating of cow slobber. As I drove from the field with my head sticking out of the window, we were escorted by a gaggle of cavorting cows, snorting, loping, and kicking around the car, all the way to the gate.

At the local service station, as the proprietor replaced the windshield wipers and I scrubbed the car windows and windshield, I gave him the details of what had just happened to our car. "Oh yeah," he casually reckoned. "You can't never leave a car in the field with a bunch of Holsteins. They're tryin' to get salt or somethin'. And if you leave your window down, they'll eat the steering wheel!" Well, now I had been warned.

My wife and I agreed on the site for the cabin, almost precisely where Aunt Vera and Uncle Neal had wanted to build their dream home. For once, Aunt Vera was pleased. But before construction began on the cabin, I thought it wise to surround the site with an electric fence. Since we had no electric power, the fence charger had to be of the battery powered type, and I soon learned that battery charged electric fences are pretty unreliable and that Holsteins check fences several times a day. We departed for the city on a Sunday afternoon, confident that we need not be concerned about cattle getting into the building site. Workers would be there all week, excavating for the foundation and putting up the cinder block walls for the basement, and what could there be on the site that the cows could harm or that could harm the cows?

We returned the following Friday evening to find the electric fence trampled into the ground and cattle taking up residence within the newly completed basement walls. About a dozen were inside, jostling one another as they competed over mutilated paper bags which had originally contained a gray powdered substance. Several forty-pound bags of mortar mix had been torn open and the Holsteins were having a feast. I called the contractor and learned that the workers had vacated the site only a few hours before we arrived and that they left behind five or six bags of mortar mix. I told my wife. "We are going to have to bury a bunch of cows."

When I contacted the owner, he was completely unworried, telling me that I underestimated the Holstein constitution. He was obviously right, because these cattle suffered no perceptible ill effects. The only long-term evidence that a couple of hundred pounds of mortar mix had been consumed by the Holsteins was a collection of very durable cow patties left scattered over the site. Years later, we were still stumbling over piles of concrete-reinforced cow poop.

Not long after the mortar eating incident, we got electric power up to the site and enclosed the area with a potent AC-powered electric fence. I assumed that our intruding cow troubles were over, but I quickly learned that Holsteins are not easily deterred. There are many unanticipated forces which can interfere with the functioning of an electric fence. It is amazing how animals which act as stupid as Holsteins do most of the time can occasionally exhibit such intelligent behavior. We would watch as a group of cows would cluster near the fence, then gang up on a low ranking member of the herd and bump it into the fence to test it. Flynn, a man with many years of experience with both animals and electric fences summed it all up. "Dogs will remember an electric fence for the rest of their lives, horses will remember for months, but Holsteins must be retrained daily."

Aunt Vera visited the family cemetery often, since it held so many of her family and now included her beloved Neal. After such visits, she would sometimes drive Neal's old truck on up the hill to visit us and deliver a complaint. Aunt Vera was always a tiny lady and she got even smaller with age. We knew she was coming when we would see an old, blue, four-wheel-drive Chevrolet truck guided by an invisible driver meandering up the hill.

"John Dear," she would address me upon her arrival, making the same old pun with my name that she had been tormenting me with since I was old enough to realize it was a pun. "Your cows have butted down another headstone and eaten the flowers I planted."

"They're not my cattle, Aunt Vera," I would remind her. "They're Flynn's. But I'll put the stone back up and fix the fence."

Planting shrubbery around the cabin provided new insight into Holstein philosophy. The field in which the Holsteins grazed was bordered with native rhododendron, a flora they studiously ignored. But any time these perverted creatures were able to breach our electric defenses, they were magnetically drawn to the hybrid purple rhododendron which we were carefully cultivating around the cabin. They didn't actually eat them; they'd just pull the bushes out of the ground, chew on them a bit, and then trample them into the earth. And while the opportunity was present, the loose-laid stone wall I had placed around the new shrubbery also had to be butted down. The more intrepid heifers would sometimes climb up the stairs onto the deck, but they inflicted little serious damage; just browsing, licking windows, pooping on porch furniture, the usual vandalism. It's all part of the Holstein philosophy, you know: "If you can't eat it or break it, poop on it."

Since cars obviously had to be kept inside the protective perimeter of the electric fence, the section of the fence across the driveway needed to be easily disconnected. We obtained an insulated handle made for just that purpose, but visitors would sometimes not see the single strand of wire across the road and drive right through it. The obvious solution was to hang a few strips of duct tape from the wire to make it more visible (duct tape use No. 2343). This stopped folks from driving through the fence, but the strips of tape kept disappearing.

I watched one day as a very large cow moseyed up the driveway and focused in on a flapping strip of tape. "This should be good," I thought, as the cow sniffed at the tape, then gave it a powerful "chomp." The loud "zap" I heard as the electrical charge arced to her tongue, was followed by a loud snort as the Holstein jumped back a few feet. The animal then adopted an aggressive stance, glaring at the offending strip of tape and shaking her lowered head. She then marched determinedly back to the fence and chomped the tape again, this time jerking back with the strip of tape clenched firmly in her teeth. She raised her head high as she turned away, chewing on the duct tape and giving a loud belch as she departed.

Eventually, I constructed a strong board fence with a sturdy metal gate to protect our cabin and yard and built a similar fence around the cemetery. This solved several problems, but then out of either frustration or boredom, the cattle began escaping through the aged barbed wire fence surrounding the field. No sooner would Flynn find and repair one hole in the fence than the cows would locate or create another, usually ending up feasting on grass and wildflowers beside the Blue Ridge Parkway.

Aunt Vera was a great help in our keeping up with the errant cattle, since both she and the Holsteins were very early risers. It became a common occurrence for me to get a phone call about 6:00 am. "John Dear," a mildly scolding, quavering voice would begin. "I'm standing here looking out of my front window, and I think those must be your cows that I see up there grazing along the Parkway. I surely would hate for someone to run into one of those big cows and get hurt."

"Thank you, Aunt Vera," I would always respond. "Don't worry, I'll take care of it." Then I would call Flynn.

The escapes became such a problem that Flynn and I agreed that there would have to be some major changes. The ancient fences had deteriorated beyond repair, and it would be quite costly to replace them. The logical solution was to give up pasturing cattle in that field and to start growing hay. That fall, Flynn sent the Holsteins to their great reward, then seeded and fertilized the field.

The following spring was warm and rainy, and the June hay crop was abundant. As he harvested the hay, Flynn carefully guided the bailer so that as each roll was ejected onto the hillside with its flat ends facing up and down the slope for stability. Sixty huge round bales, each consisting of a half-ton of high-grade Timothy hay were scattered over our mountain meadow. We were well pleased with our decision to grow hay instead of cattle. "Good deal, man," grinned Flynn, as he jumped down from his tractor to give me a high-five. "A super crop of hay here, and we don't have to worry about hay bales breaking out through the fence."

The next morning, I was awakened by a 6:00 a.m. telephone call and greeted by a familiar voice. "John Dear," the accusing, quavering complaint began, "I am here looking out of my front window, and I think that it must be your hay bale that I see up there lying in the middle of the Parkway. I surely would hate for someone to run into that big old hay roll and get hurt."

The Old Damon Road

The Road

"Grandma, why aren't there any children in Virginia?"

"There are lots of children in Virginia," my wife assured our seven-year-old grandson. "There just aren't many around here."

"Well then, why aren't there any children in Mayberry?"

"They're probably in school today. They are on a different school schedule in this county."

"But there aren't any children at church, and that's on Sunday. And they don't come to the store either."

Scotty was almost right. There are only a very few children in Mayberry. In fact, there are very few people of child-bearing age in Mayberry. If the membership of Mayberry Presbyterian Church is a valid statistical sample, most of the residents of Mayberry are drawing Social Security. There actually are a few children in Mayberry, but a very few, and there are likely to be even fewer in the foreseeable future.

"How much longer will there even be a Mayberry?" I began to wonder.

But right then, I was instructed to get the children out of the house for a while. Our two grandsons, ages seven and ten, are really good kids, but the weather had been cool and drizzly for the last couple of days. The boys, visiting us in Mayberry over their spring school break, had been stuck in the house most of the time and were getting really rambunctious. They are, after all, little boys with a lot of energy, and now they had been chasing each other around inside the house, jumping over the furniture while making shooting and crashing and dive bomber noises. Little boys can play only so many games of Jenga or checkers, and their normally sweet and patient grandmother was suffering from frayed nerves. Fortunately, the weather was improving.

The boys really like coming to Mayberry and doing all the things that mountain boys have done for hundreds of years: hiking over the hills, climbing over the fences, swinging on the gate (which they have expressly been told not to do), climbing the apple trees, exploring the woods, shooting their sling shots, and creating hideaways in the laurel thickets. Until recently, whenever the boys began to wear on us inside the house, we would just tell them to go outside and play. But that was before the bears showed up.

Now, whenever they go outside of the yard, their grandmother has decreed that I have to accompany them. Not that I would be of much use in a bear attack, except that the boys can run faster than their old grandpa, so the bear would get me instead of one of them. That, I think, is their grandmother's logic.

Living up here as a kid, the only bear I ever saw was in Rocky Knob National Park, and that was only a year or two after the government first released them. I used to listen to "the old folks" tell snake tales, wild hog tales, and panther tales. But I don't recall ever hearing one of them tell of a local adventure involving a bear.

Although bears come around a lot more often than they used to, they really don't seem very threatening. In my two face-to-face bear encounters, once when a bear was munching on the bird feeder out in the front yard, and then again when one was scoffing up apples in the orchard, I shouted and waved my arms and the bear just left. In neither case, however, did the bear seem to be in any great hurry; it would just sort of casually saunter into the surrounding woods, looking back at me as if to let me know that he really wouldn't have to leave if he didn't choose to. Not too long ago, my wife yelled and waved her arms at a bear that was checking out the grill on the patio, and the result was the same.

If I try to go into the woods directly behind our house, I encounter the obstacle of what my dad used to call a laurel hell. To get through it, I have to pull and push and break rhododendron limbs, all while threshing and crashing about and making a great fuss. The bears, however, large as they are, seem to easily merge into the rhododendron thicket anywhere they choose, silently melting off into the woods. That I find to be rather scary.

So the big problem was finding something for the boys to do outside, something that would keep them happy and occupied for a good long while. With the ground still partially frozen and wet and mushy, our options were seriously limited. We could either walk down the lane to the Mayberry Trading Post or we could take a walk on *the old road*.

When presented with the two choices, the boys reminded me that they had been to The Trading Post just the day before and spent all their money. That left the second option, about which they were even less enthusiastic. Then I thought of a project that might interest them for now and maybe keep them busy on future visits.

"Guys, you're always wanting to build a fire outside to roast hot dogs and marshmallows. Maybe we need to build a fire pit." Although I think they really didn't know what I meant by a fire pit, that suggestion was met with great enthusiasm anyway.

"Yes, yes, lets build a fire pit! Grandma! Grandpa says we can build a fire pit!" followed by, "How do we do that, Grandpa?"

"Well, we will need a lot of rocks. So the first thing we need to do is to look for rocks. After we have found and piled up a bunch of rocks, then we'll have to decide where to build it. When we decide on a location, we'll dig up a circle in the sod, put down a layer of flat rocks, and then build a little rock wall around the outside."

"How many rocks do we need?"

I had not given the project much thought before proposing it, so I was playing by ear at this point. "Oh, about a hundred, I guess."

"What kind of rocks? Where will we get the rocks?"

"Well, there are plenty of rocks all around here, but we will need a lot of rocks of just the right size. We will need some flat ones about the size of a book and some square ones about the size of your head. And I happen to know where there are plenty of rocks to choose from."

"I know, I know!" shouted Scottie, jumping onto and off of the sofa. "The old road. We can get lots of rocks from the old road."

That was exactly what I had in mind.

Getting onto the old road simply requires a short hike up the hill through the orchard and a quick scramble along a pathway we have cut through the rhododendron thicket. Along the section of the old road near our house, the rhododendron have grown up on either side of the road and together over the top, forming a canopy that prevents any vegetation from growing in the old road bed beneath. Once you break through the rhododendron thicket and get onto the old road, the tunnel it forms extends as far as you can see in either direction. You can turn to the left and

follow the tunnel down the hill for almost half a mile and
come out at the Blue Ridge Parkway. Or you can turn to
the right and follow the road for about a half mile along the
ridge. In that direction, west, the old road ends at a fence
that marks the boundary of a cousin's property and also the
county line. From the fence, you can see across a corn field
to the beginning of *Trail Road*, originally a continuation of
the old road. It goes all the way to Terry's Mill Road and to
a community once known as Bankstown.

It only takes a few minutes to walk through the
orchard to the top of the hill and then slip and slide through
the rhododendron thicket to the edge of the old road. We
know that we have arrived when we come upon a small
sign nailed to a tree informing us that the property we are
about to enter belongs to the Department of the Interior.
The old road pretty much marks the boundary between our
land and several hundred acres which were bought up by
the Federal Government during the Nixon Administration.

The sky has cleared and the sun is shining, but it is
dark, damp, and chilly inside the rhododendron tunnel. As
soon as we get on the old road, the boys turn right, shouting
and running along the road to the West, the exact opposite
of the direction I intended to go. Still, I am in no hurry with
our project. The main objective is to get the boys out of the
house and keep them out of their grandmother's way for as
long as possible.

It's a windy day, but as usual, there is no wind
blowing inside the rhododendron tunnel. Walking as fast as
I can while breathlessly calling to the boys to wait up, I
have to step over something in the road that looks a lot like
bear scat to me. As the boys run ahead and I try to keep
within shouting distance, I make mental notes of our
progress as we pass old familiar landmarks. There is the

intersection of our old road with a rutted trench that my
grandpa always called the Sam Vipperman Road, then we
pass a pile of rock representing the collapsed chimney that
was once a part of Jule Boswell's cabin. The boys stop at
the pile of chimney rubble and begin kicking and scraping
the leaves off of a pile of very large stones. "How about
these rocks, Grandpa?"

When I tell them those rocks are much too large,
they are off to the races again. When they come to the
fence and the obvious end of the road, they climb up on the
fence and wait for me. Before I can get my breath, they
begin to pepper me with questions.

"Grandpa, why is there a road out here in the
middle of the woods, where nobody lives? Did people used
to drive cars over this road? Does this road have a name,
like *Squirrel Spur* or *Kettle Hollow*?"

After I have caught my breath, I try to give them
some answers.

"Well, the road just passes through this big patch of
woods right here. It is a part of the road that used to run all
the way from Meadows of Dan to Bankstown. Mayberry
has not always been so covered with woods. Most of this
was cleared land when I was a kid."

"A long time ago, there were houses all along this
road. See that level spot over there?" I am pointing up the
hollow towards Hurricane Knob. "My family always called
this the Damon Road because a man named Damon
Barnard used to have a big house beside the road right
there. But that house burned down fifty or sixty years ago.
I think Grover Young's family lived there then."

"Remember the ruins of the cabin where you found
the pile of chimney stones? My mother could remember
when a woman named Julia Boswell lived there, and her

cabin was not in the middle of the woods then. Mom could remember that the cabin stood in an open field. She said the cabin had a rough little picket fence around it. Aunt Jule they called her, had flowers planted in her yard, hydrangeas and day lilies. She had a vegetable garden next to the cabin and her little corn field ran up the hill beside the road."

"But people like Julia Boswell all moved away or died, and no one took their place. People can't make a living on a small farm anymore. There were about three hundred people living in Mayberry when your Great Grandmother Mac lived here; there are about twenty-five now. And I think there are only four houses from those days that are still standing."

"This road has had several names. Some folks called it The Terry Road, some called it The Bankstown Road, and I have even heard it called The Old Pike. But every one of the old folks I ever asked about this road was sure that it has been here for a very long time. Just how long, no one is sure, probably more than two hundred years. Over that time, it has been known by a lot of names."

I begin herding the boys back down the road toward the east, the direction I had originally intended for us to go. "We can't find rocks like we need up here. Now we need to walk way down the road towards the Parkway."

The boys had stopped listening to me some time ago. As soon as we get back to the rhododendron tunnel, they run on ahead, laughing and yelling. There will be no bear coming around here with all that noise.

Near the eastern end of the tunnel, where the rhododendron become sparse, the road traverses a stepped rock bluff. There the little guys entertain themselves by climbing up and down and scrambling across the bluff's narrow ledges. The rock is damp and mossy, and I am concerned that they might slip, but I refrain from cautioning them. Their grandmother and I continually tell them to be careful, to the point where it has little effect.

As I start down the steep hill from the tunnel, I enter a section of the road where the road bed is five or six feet below the surrounding land and the road is bordered on either side by a rocky berm, rocks piled upon rocks, rocks of just the size we are looking for. "Hey guys, " I call to the grandkids. "Here is what we are looking for."

The boys are intently occupied with their exploration of the rock bluff and either don't hear me or they choose to ignore me. That's okay. I'll just let them burn off a little more energy while I look around.

The berms are not natural formations. These rocky banks were created by thoughtful travelers. As a rock of significant size became exposed by traffic and erosion, someone walking along this road would pick it up and carry it out of the way to make the way smoother for future travelers. Moving a large rock out of the way might keep it from breaking a wagon wheel. How many years would it take for this many rocks to be removed from the road and piled five feet high along the sides? I really don't know, but I would guess a hundred, maybe two.

The trees are bare of leaves this time of year, so from this high point, I can visually track the old road all of the way down the hill to the Parkway and beyond. I can follow its path down the hill from the far side of the Parkway to the Mayberry Road, where there is a short section of the old road that is still used to get farm equipment across the Parkway and in and out of the field beside where I stand.

On the far side of Mayberry Road, there is a paved road, once called Cold Spring Road and now renamed

Mayberry Creek Road. It mostly follows the original route of this old road we are on, down across Mayberry Creek and up and around the hill on the other side. It reappears in the distance, at the top of the hill near the Spangler Cemetery and soon disappears again, but I know its path by heart. I know that about another mile to the east, near the community once known as Tobax, a private drive turns off and meanders across the base of *The Knobs*. That drive is a remnant of what used to be known as the Wildcat Road, a road which was an extension of the Rye Cove Road, the westward route up the mountain from Stuart.

I am looking down on the last leg of the long day's journey my great grandmother and her little brood first traveled when they came to Mayberry, over one hundred and thirty years ago. Below me, right at the foot of the hill beside Mayberry Creek, I think I can just make out the faint imprint of a narrow lane that once turned off of the Cold Spring Road and ran south along beside Mayberry Creek, past Wolford Spangler's grist mill and into a rocky hollow. That is where, five generations before my grandsons, Muh and her family settled in a borrowed cabin, where they scraped, scratched, and barely survived their first years here in these mountains.

With more strength and more resources, Muh and her family might have kept on moving along this road, on to Bankstown, maybe on to Wytheville. They could have conceivably continued on to Abingdon or Charleston, possibly into Kentucky or Ohio and on to the West.

But they did not. Most likely, they could not. Uncertain and weary, the family ended the journey there beside the creek. And put down their roots in Mayberry.

Mayberry, Virginia

Pamela Watts

A place where home can be dreamed:
Where hummingbirds hang like private paintings
Against a backdrop of the Blue Ridge Mountains,
Muted and blue, by the mist;

Where relatives spill like drops of sea water
Down a front porch chattering,
The smell of fried chicken and peach cobbler
Wafting across the grass;
Where the same stories have been told so often,
They brush the skin softly and loose;
Where Great-grands take the time
To teach the meaning of "once removed."

I can imagine, as I watch the babies
Become toddlers, become kidlets,
In a process like time-lapse photography,
That this is a tribe
Where cousins bring potentials to audition for the Aunts,
Then marry, have babies;
That this is my tribe,
My blossoming family tree,
That I belong someplace

Simple;
Where I once bought a popsicle for a nickel.

81845609R00121

Made in the USA
Lexington, KY
22 February 2018